The ESSENT[IALS]

Psychology II

Linda Leal, Ph.D.
Associate Professor, Department of Psychology
Eastern Illinois University – Charleston, Illinois

Research & Education Association
Visit our website at
www.rea.com

Research & Education Association
61 Ethel Road West
Piscataway, New Jersey 08854
E-mail: info@rea.com

THE ESSENTIALS®
OF PSYCHOLOGY II

Year 2006 Printing

Printed in the United States of America

Library of Congress Control Number 2001086395

International Standard Book Number 0-87891-931-7

What REA's Essentials®
Will Do for You

This book is part of REA's celebrated *Essentials*® series of review and study guides, relied on by tens of thousands of students over the years for being complete yet concise.

Here you'll find a summary of the very material you're most likely to need for exams, not to mention homework—eliminating the need to read and review many pages of textbook and class notes.

This slim volume condenses the vast amount of detail characteristic of the subject matter and summarizes the **essentials** of the field. The book provides quick access to the important definitions, principles, practices, and theories in the field.

It will save you hours of study and preparation time.

This *Essentials*® book has been prepared by experts in the field and has been carefully reviewed to ensure its accuracy and maximum usefulness. We believe you'll find it a valuable, handy addition to your library.

Larry B. Kling
Chief Editor

Contents

Chapter 3
ASSESSING INTELLIGENCE AND PERSONALITY

Chapter 4
MOTIVATION AND EMOTION

Chapter 5
ABNORMAL BEHAVIOR

Chapter 6
PSYCHOTHERAPY

Chapter 7
SOCIAL BEHAVIOR

CHAPTER 1

Human Development

1.1 Physical and Perceptual Development

Developmental psychologists study age-related changes that occur throughout the life span, from conception until death. Traditionally, developmental psychologists have focused on childhood, but other periods of development are studied as well.

The **nature vs. nurture** debate has motivated the study of development. That is, is a person's development determined by **heredity** or by **environment**? Psychologists today recognize that both nature and nurture interact to influence the developmental process.

Heredity is the transmission of ancestor characteristics from parents to offspring through the genes. **Genes** determine hereditary characteristics and are the chemical blueprints of all living things. Genes are made up of **DNA** or **deoxyribonucleic acid** and possess the information that determines the makeup of every cell in our body. Genes lie along **chromosomes**, bodies that are in the nucleus of each cell in our body. Every human body cell (except the sex cells) contains **46** chromosomes arranged in **23 pairs**.

The **sex cells** (**ova** or egg cell in the female and **sperm** in the male) contain **23 single** chromosomes. Fertilization results in **23 pairs** of chromosomes—one member of each pair is contributed by the mother, the other by the father.

Every female egg contains an **X chromosome** and every male sperm cell contains *either* an **X** or a **Y chromosome**. At conception, if the egg is fertilized by a sperm carrying a Y chromosome, the

1

offspring will be **XY** or male. If the egg is fertilized by a sperm carrying an X chromosome, the child will be **XX** or female.

Genotype is a term used to refer to an individual's genetic make-up.

Phenotype refers to how a given genotype is expressed (i.e., what the person looks like or how the person behaves). Phenotype occurs as a result of an interaction between genotype and environment.

Dominant genes are expressed in an individual's phenotype whenever they are present in the genotype. **Recessive genes** are expressed in an individual's phenotype only when they are paired with a similar recessive gene.

1.1.1 Prenatal Development

Prenatal development refers to the period of development from conception to birth. The average pregnancy lasts 270 days or 40 weeks.

At conception, the **female egg** or **ovum** is fertilized by the **male sperm,** usually in the **Fallopian tube.** This results in a **fertilized egg** that is called a **zygote.** The zygote repeatedly divides as it travels down the Fallopian tube to the **uterus,** where it becomes attached to the uterine wall.

The three stages of prenatal development are outlined below:

Ovum or **Germinal**	The first two weeks after conception. Is a microscopic mass of multiplying cells. Zygote travels down Fallopian tube and implants itself on the wall of the uterus. **Placenta** (provides nourishment and allows wastes to pass out to the mother) begins to form. **Umbilical cord** carries nourishment from and waste to the placenta. Thin membranes keep fetal and maternal bloodstreams separate.
Embryo	Second to eighth week after conception. Only about one inch long by end of this stage. Most vital organs and bodily systems *begin* to form. Major birth defects are often

2

due to problems that occur during this stage. **Amniotic sac**, or fluid-filled sac, surrounds embryo to serve as protection and provide a constant temperature.

Fetus From two months after conception until birth. Muscles and bones form. Vital organs continue to grow and begin to function. During last three months, brain develops rapidly.

An outline of *what* develops *when* during the prenatal period is as follows:

Approximate prenatal week	Development
2nd week	Implantation on uterine wall.
3rd – 4th week	Heart begins to pump.
4th week	Digestive system begins to form. Eyes begin to form.
5th week	Ears begin to form.
6th week	Arms and legs first begin to appear.
7th – 8th week	Male sex organs form. Fingers form.
8th week	Bones begin to form. Legs and arms move. Toes form.
10th – 11th week	Female sex organs form.
12th week	Fetus weighs about one ounce. Fetal movement can occur. Fingerprints form.
20th week	Mother feels movement. Reflexes—sucking, swallowing, and hiccuping appear. Nails, sweat glands, and soft hair developing.

27th week	Fetus weighs about two pounds.
38th week	Fetus weighs about seven pounds.
40th week	Full-term baby born.

Teratogens are any agents that may cross the placental barrier from mother to embryo/fetus, causing abnormalities. What abnormalities occur depend on what is developing prenatally as well as what the harmful agent is. Possible teratogens include maternal diseases, diet, drug use (including alcohol and nicotine), exposure to X-rays, and other environmental influences. For instance, **fetal alcohol syndrome** (i.e., short nose, thin upper lip, widely spaced eyes, small head, mental retardation) can occur as a result of alcohol consumption during pregnancy.

Because so many vital organs and body parts are developing during the **embryo stage**, harmful agents are especially dangerous during this prenatal period. This is often referred to as a **critical period** in development. A critical period is any time during development that some developmental process must occur or it never will. For example, if something interferes with legs developing or forming prenatally, they will not develop or be formed later.

1.1.2 Perceptual Development

The five senses, although not fully developed, are functional at birth. For instance, infants can **hear** prior to birth. Shortly after birth, newborn infants or **neonates** appear capable of discriminating between sounds of different duration, loudness, and pitch. Newborns also appear to prefer the sound of a human voice. By six months of age, infants can discriminate between any two basic sounds used in language. In fact, they can make distinctions between sounds that older children and adults can no longer make because these sounds are not heard in their spoken language.

The sense of **smell** is also well developed in the newborn. By six weeks of age, infants can smell the difference between their mothers and strangers.

Infants respond to the four basic **tastes** (sweet, sour, salty, and bitter), but they usually prefer sweet.

Infants are also responsive to **touch**. Some research has shown that female infants may be more sensitive to touch than males. One area of study related to touch in young infants is the study of reflexes.

A number of **reflexes** (involuntary responses to stimuli) can be elicited in newborn infants. All healthy newborns exhibit them and many of these reflexes will disappear with age. For example, healthy newborn infants will blink when a light shines in their eyes. This reflex does not disappear with time. But other reflexes, such as the **Moro** (extension of arms when infant feels a loss of support), **Palmar** (hand grasp), and **Rooting** (turns toward object brushing cheek and attempts to suck) will disappear over the course of the first year of life.

At birth, neonates can see although their **visual acuity** is very poor (about 20/400 to 20/800 compared to average adult visual acuity of 20/20). Newborn infants can focus best on objects that are about nine inches away. They can also follow a moving object. Young infants also prefer to see the human face and other visual stimuli that have contour, contrast, complexity, and movement. By the time infants can crawl, they indicate that they have **depth perception** by refusing to crawl across the deep side of a **visual cliff**.

1.1.3 Motor Development

Maturation is a term used to describe a genetically programmed biological plan of development that is relatively independent of experience.

The **proximodistal principle** of development describes the center-outward direction of motor development. For instance, children gain control of their torso before their extremities (e.g., they can sit independently before they can stand).

The **cephalocaudal principle** describes the head-to-foot direction of motor development. That is, children tend to gain control over the upper portions of their bodies before the lower part (e.g., they can reach and grasp before they can walk).

Developmental norms describe the average age that children display various abilities.

The developmental norms for motor development are as follows:

Age	Behavior
1 month	While prone (on stomach), can lift head.
2 months	While prone, can hold chest up. Can roll from side to back.
3 months	Can roll over. Will reach for objects.
6 – 7 months	Sits without support. Stands holding on to objects.
8 – 10 months	Crawls.
8 – 12 months	Pulls self up to stand.
11 – 12 months	"Cruises"—walks by holding on to objects.
12 – 18 months	Walks alone.

1.2 Social Development

Children also grow socially as they develop.

1.2.1 Temperament

Temperament refers to a child's characteristic mood and activity level. Even young infants are temperamentally different from one another.

The New York Longitudinal Study (1956), carried out by **Stella Chess, Alexander Thomas**, and **Herbert Birch**, is a research project that investigated temperament.

A **longitudinal** study is one that repeatedly observes and follows-up the same group of individuals as they mature. For example, a group of children could have their temperament assessed when they are three months old, and again when they are two years old, five years old, and 10 years old.

A **cross-sectional** study studies different groups of individuals who are at different ages at the same point in time. A group of three–month–olds, two–year–olds, and five–year–olds may be assessed for temperament. In cross-sectional studies, therefore, the same individuals are not retested but instead are measured only once and group averages are used to demonstrate developmental changes.

The New York Longitudinal Study followed 140 children from birth to adolescence. Thomas, Chess, and Birch interviewed parents when the infants were between two and three months of age and rated the infants based on **activity level, rhythmicity, approach/ withdrawal, adaptability, intensity of reaction,** and **quality of mood**. Thomas et al. found that they could classify infants into different groups based on temperament:

Easy Infants (40%)	Adaptable to new situations. Predictable in their rhythmicity or schedule. Positive in their mood.
Difficult Infants (10%)	Intense in their reactions. Not very adaptable to new situations. Slightly negative mood. Irregular body rhythms.
Slow-to-warm–up Infants (15%)	Initially withdraw when approached, but may later "warm up." Slow to adapt to new situations.
Average Infants (35%)	Did not fit into any of the above categories.

Thomas et al. found that temperament was fairly stable over time. For instance, they found that 70% of the difficult infants developed behavior problems during childhood, while only 18% of the easy infants did so. There were, of course, individual differences in whether specific children showed continuity or dramatic changes in their temperament over time.

Although early temperament appears to be highly biologically determined, environment can also influence temperament. Researchers have used the term **goodness of fit** to describe an environment where an infant's temperament matches the opportunities, expectations, and demands the infant encounters.

7

1.2.2 Attachment

Attachment is the close emotional relationship between an infant and her or his caretakers.

Initially, infants attempt to attract the attention (usually through crying, smiling, etc.) of no one in particular. Eventually infants develop the ability to discriminate familiar from unfamiliar people. Shortly thereafter, they may cry or otherwise become distressed when preferred caregivers leave the room. This is referred to as **separation anxiety**. Separation anxiety may begin as early as 6 months of age, but it usually peaks around 18 months and then gradually declines.

Mary Ainsworth and her colleagues found they could distinguish three categories of attachments based on the quality of the infant-caregiver interactions.

Secure Attachments	Children use parent as **secure base** from which they explore their environment. They become upset if parent leaves the room but are glad to see the parent when parent returns.
Insecure Attachments	
Anxious-Ambivalent	Tend not to use parent as a secure base (and may often cling or refuse to leave parent). They become very upset when parent leaves and may often appear angry or become more upset when parent returns.
Avoidant	These children seek little contact with parent and are not concerned when parent leaves. Usually avoid interaction when parent returns.

Parents of securely attached infants are often found to be more sensitive and responsive to their child's needs.

Some studies have found a relationship between attachment patterns and children's later adjustment. For instance, one study found that securely attached infants were less frustrated and happier at two years of age than were their insecurely attached peers.

Some researchers have suggested that temperament, genetic characteristics, and "goodness of fit" may be important for both the type of attachment bond formed and a child's later developmental outcome.

1.2.3 Parenting Styles

Diana Baumrind found that she could classify parents according to the following:

Authoritative Parents	Affectionate and loving. Provide control when necessary and set limits. Allow children to express their own point of view—engage in "verbal give and take." Their children tend to be self-reliant, competent, and socially responsible.
Authoritarian Parents	Demand unquestioning obedience. Use punishment to control behavior. Less likely to be affectionate. Their children tend to be unhappy, distrustful, ineffective in social interactions, and often become dependent adults.
Permissive Parents	Make few demands. Allow children to make their own decisions. Use inconsistent discipline. Their children tend to be immature, lack self-control, and explore less.

1.2.4 Day Care

Even though more children than ever before are attending day care, there have been relatively few well-controlled studies that have looked at the effects of day care on development. Summarized below are the most consistent findings to date.

Children who attend day care usually score higher than children who do not attend day care on tests of **intelligence**. Non-day care children, however, usually catch up once they enter kindergarten and elementary school.

Children in day care tend to be more **socially skilled**—more cooperative, more confident, and better able to take the perspective of another.

Day care children also tend to be more **aggressive** and **noncompliant** (less likely to carry out an adult's request). Some have suggested this is because day care children have learned to think for themselves, not a symptom of maladjustment.

There is a slight tendency for day care children to be classified as **insecurely attached** (36% vs. 29% for home care children). Although statistically significant, some have questioned the practical significance of a 7% difference.

1.3 Gender Role Development

Gender roles are our set of expectations about appropriate activities for females and males. Research has shown that even preschoolers believe that males and females have different characteristics. They also believe it is inappropriate to act like a member of the other gender.

Theories that explain gender role development include:

Social Learning Theory	Proposes that children learn gender roles because they are **rewarded** for appropriate behavior and **punished** for inappropriate gender role behaviors. Children also watch and **imitate** the behaviors of others.
Cognitive Theory	**Kohlberg** argued that children learn about gender the same way that they acquire other cognitive concepts (see Piaget's theory described below). First, preschool children acquire **gender identity**—that is, they

identify themselves as male or female. Then children **classify** others, activities, objects, etc. as male or female. Once these gender concepts are acquired, children engage in **gender-typed behavior**— they prefer same-gender playmates, activities, etc. Kohlberg also proposed that preschool children lack **gender constancy**. That is, they do not understand that a person's gender stays the same despite changes in outward physical appearance.

Psychoanalytic or Freud's Theory

Freud's theory (see chapter 2) proposes that children establish their gender-role identity as a result of **identification with their same-sex parent** during the **Phallic stage**.

1.4 Cognitive Development

The most rapid cognitive development takes place during the first few years of life when the brain is growing rapidly. As the following sections on Piaget's theory and memory development indicate, however, cognitive development is best described as a life-long process.

1.4.1 Piaget's Theory

The Swiss researcher and writer **Jean Piaget** (1896 – 1980) spent most of his adult life describing the cognitive development of children. Although Piaget was never trained as a psychologist (his formal schooling was in biology and zoology), his theory of cognitive development has had a dramatic impact on how we view the abilities of children.

Piaget felt that cognitive development proceeded through four stages: the **sensorimotor stage** lasts from birth to approximately 18 months of age, the **preoperational stage** lasts from two to seven years of age, the stage of **concrete operations** covers the years seven to twelve, and finally, **formal operations**, extends from twelve years on.

According to Piaget, the order in which children pass through these stages is **invariant** or does not vary. The rate at which children pass through these stages does vary from child to child.

Piaget wrote that each stage of cognitive development represents a **qualitatively** different way of thinking. That is, children in each stage think differently from children in the other stages. Therefore, it is not just that children acquire more information as they grow older, but *how* they think actually changes with age.

Children pass from one stage to another as a result of **biological maturity** and **experiences** in their environment.

The major characteristics of each of these four stages follow:

Sensorimotor Stage

Children "think" during this stage as a result of coordination of sensory input and motor responses. Because the child has not developed language, intelligence is nonverbal or **nonsymbolic** (the child cannot mentally represent objects or events). This stage is divided into **six substages** that outline how cognitive development proceeds during this stage. These six substages also represent the development of **object permanence**. Piaget was the first to suggest that infants lack object permanence—that is, they cannot mentally represent or think about objects that they are not directly interacting with (or, put another way, "out of sight, out of mind").

Preoperational Stage

Preoperational thinkers can now **symbolize** or mentally represent their world. They can now think about objects that they are not interacting with at the present time. This period is dominated by a rapid development of **language,** which is a form of symbolic thinking. Children do have several limitations during this stage, however. These include **irreversibility** or the inability to mentally reverse a physical action to return an object to its original stage, **centration** (tendency to focus on one detail in a situation to the neglect of other important features), and **egocentrism** (inability to consider another's viewpoint). These three limitations are used to describe why preoperational children cannot solve **conservation tasks** (i.e., they do not understand that quantity cannot be judged by appearance alone.). A preoperational child might believe that when you pour water from a tall, thin glass into a wide-mouthed, shorter glass, you have less water. The child centrates attention on the appearance of more water and cannot mentally reverse the operation and think about pouring the water back into the tall, thin glass.

Concrete Operations
During concrete operations, children understand conservation. They understand, for example, that when water is poured from a tall, thin glass into a wide-mouthed, shorter glass, there is the same amount of water. Concrete operational children, therefore, can **decenter** their attention and understand **reversibility**. Concrete thinkers can also **arrange objects** according to size or weight and can **divide** something **into** its **parts**. **Mathematical operations** develop during this stage. Children are limited in this stage because thinking can only be applied to **concrete objects** and **events**, and they will have difficulty dealing with **hypothetical problems**.

Formal Operations
Formal operational thinkers can handle **hypothetical problems**. They are, for instance, able to project themselves into the future and think about long-term goals. **Scientific reasoning** is also possible. That is, the ability to isolate a problem, review it systematically, and figure out all possible solutions is evident. The formal thinker is capable of understanding and appreciating the **symbolic abstractions** of algebra and literary criticism as well as the use of **metaphor** in literature. Formal operations, therefore, involve the development of **logical** and **systematic thinking**.

Other key terms from Piaget's theory include:

Scheme or **Schema**   Basic thought structures about what the world, objects, events, etc. are like.

Organization	Combining and integrating simple schemes.
Adaptation	Modifying existing schemes to fit new experiences. Consists of **assimilation** and **accommodation**.
Assimilation	Interpreting an event or experience based on our current scheme or thought structure. (For example, a child who calls all four-legged animals—even cats—"doggie." This child's current scheme seems to be that if you have fur and four legs, you are a dog.)
Accommodation	Changing or adjusting a scheme based on experience, understanding, etc. (e.g., the above mentioned child's dog scheme accommodates or adjusts to the notion that at least some four-legged animals are "cats.").

Criticisms of Piaget's theory include his underestimation of children's cognitive abilities. Studies have shown that children are capable of performing many tasks (e.g., conservation) at earlier ages than Piaget predicted. Piaget also paid little attention to individual differences. Some aspects of his theory (e.g., formal operations) may be culturally specific.

1.4.2 Memory Development

Over the course of development, children use more and more sophisticated methods to remember, and their memory performance improves as a result. Although young infants (before three months of age) demonstrate memory capability when they recognize and remember familiar people, smells, objects, etc., in their environment, the use of intentional strategies for remembering have not been documented until around two years of age. These early strategies for remembering include **looking, pointing**, and **naming**.

By early elementary school, children are using **rehearsal** as a method for remembering. Rehearsal is a generic term for a variety of memory strategies that involve **repetition** as a method for remembering (e.g., repeating the phone number over and over until you dial it, writing your spelling words ten times each).

Organization or **clustering** strategies develop by late elementary school and involve the semantic grouping of materials into meaningful units (e.g., grouping spelling words by their prefix).

Elaborative strategies involve creating verbal or visual connections that add meaning to material and do not develop until adolescence or later. An example would be creating the phrase "Every good boy does fine" to remember that "e," "g," "b," "d," and "f" are the lines of the treble clef in music.

Metamemory is one's knowledge about memory, and it has been divided into **person** (everything we know about the memory abilities of ourselves and others), **task** (everything we know about memory tasks), and **strategy** (everything we know about techniques of learning and remembering) factors. As with strategy use, metamemory improves with age during childhood. At first, young children are unrealistic and make overly optimistic predictions about their memories (i.e., they believe they can remember everything!) and with age they become more realistic in their expectations. They also know more about possible strategies for remembering with age.

1.5 Erikson's Psychosocial Stages of Development

Erik Erikson proposed eight stages of social-emotional/personality development. He is one of the few theorists to discuss development throughout the life span—infancy through old age.

Erikson was trained as a psychoanalytic or Freudian theorist (see chapter 2). Erikson's theory, however, is very different from Freud's. For instance, Erikson believed that personality continues to develop over the entire life span (and not just childhood). Also, Erikson does not stress unconscious motives or desires. Like Freud, Erikson did feel that events that occur early in development can leave a permanent mark on one's later social-emotional development.

A description of Erikson's eight stages of psychosocial development follows. Each stage represents a specific task or dilemma that must be resolved.

Trust versus Mistrust (First year of life)	Infant's needs must be met by responsive, sensitive caretakers. If this occurs, a basic sense of trust and optimism develops. If not, mistrust and fear of the future results.
Autonomy versus Shame and Doubt (1 – 3 years)	Children begin to express self-control by climbing, exploring, touching, and toilet training. Parents can foster a sense of autonomy by encouraging children to try new things. If restrained or punished too harshly, shame and doubt can develop.
Initiative versus Guilt (3 – 5 years)	Children are asked to assume more responsibility. Through play, children learn to plan, undertake, and carry out a task. Parents can encourage initiative by giving children the freedom to play, to use their imagination, etc. Children who are criticized or discouraged from taking the initiative, learn to feel guilty.
Industry versus Inferiority (6 – 12 years)	In elementary school, children learn skills that are valued by society. Success or failure while learning these skills can have lasting effects on a child's feelings of adequacy.
Identity versus Role Confusion (Adolescence)	The development of identity involves finding out who we are, what we value, and where we are headed in life. In their search for identity, adolescents experiment with different roles. If we establish an integrated image of ourselves as

16

	a unique person, then we establish a sense of identity. If not, role confusion results and can be expressed by individuals withdrawing and isolating themselves from family and friends or by losing themselves in the crowd.
Intimacy versus Isolation (Young Adulthood)	After establishing an identity, a person is prepared to form deep, intimate relationships with others. Failure to establish intimacy with others leads to a deep sense of isolation.
Generativity versus Stagnation (Middle Adulthood)	An interest in guiding the next generation is the main task of middle adulthood. This can be accomplished through one's creative or productive work or through caring for children. If adults do not feel that they have assisted the younger generation, a sense of stagnation will result.
Integrity versus Despair (Late Adulthood)	This is a time of looking back at our lives. If we believe, overall, our lives have been well spent, a sense of integrity develops. If not, a sense of despair over the value of one's life will result.

1.6 Kohlberg's Theory of Moral Development

Lawrence Kohlberg developed a model of moral development based on an individual's responses to moral questions called **moral dilemmas**.

Kohlberg's theory attempts to explain how children develop a sense of **right or wrong**. Kohlberg was influenced by **Piaget's** theory and therefore felt that moral development was determined by cognitive development. Figure 1.6 charts an example of Kohlberg's theory.

Kohlberg's theory describes how individuals pass through a series of **three levels of moral development**, each of which can be broken into **two sublevels**, resulting in a total of **six stages**.

Level I. Preconventional Morality

Stage 1. Punishment orientation — A person complies with rules during this stage in order to avoid punishment.

Stage 2. Reward orientation — An action is determined by one's own needs.

Level II. Conventional Morality

Stage 3. Good-girl/Good-boy orientation — Good behavior is that which pleases others and gets their approval.

Stage 4. Authority orientation — Emphasis is on upholding the law, order, and authority and doing one's duty by following societal rules.

Level III. Postconventional Morality

Stage 5. Social contract orientation — Flexible understanding that people obey rules because they are necessary for the social order but that rules can change if there are good reasons and better alternatives.

Stage 6. Morality of individual principles orientation — Behavior is directed by self-chosen ethical principles. High value is placed on justice, dignity, and equality.

Mean percent of moral statements on Kohlberg's three levels made by boys aged 7 to 16

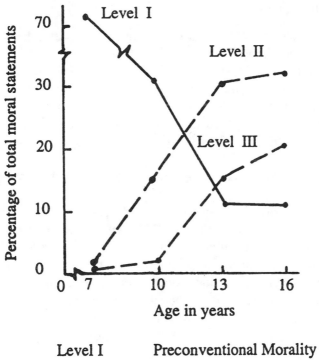

Level I   Preconventional Morality
Level II   Conventional Morality
Level III   Postconventional Morality

Figure 1.6

Criticisms of Kohlberg's theory of moral development include that it may be better at describing the development of male morality than of female morality, and development may not be as orderly and uniform as his theory suggests. For instance, it is not unusual to find individuals who are reasoning at several adjacent levels of moral reasoning at the same time. Also, Kohlberg's theory describes moral reasoning but does not predict moral behavior.

1.7 Adolescence

Adolescence is that time in development that occurs between childhood and adulthood.

Physical Changes: **Puberty** refers to rapid physical growth that occurs with hormonal changes that bring sexual maturity. **Secondary sex characteristics** (the physical features associated with gender but not directly involved in reproduction, such as male facial hair) emerge at this time. **Menarche** refers to girls' first menstrual period.

The peak growth spurt during puberty occurs earlier for girls than for boys.

Social Concerns: The main task for adolescents is to establish an identity. Adolescents are in **Erikson's identity versus role confusion** stage. Adolescents enter what Erikson called a **psychosocial moratorium,** which relates to the gap between the security of childhood and the autonomy of adulthood, where a person is free from responsibilities and can experiment with different roles.

At the turn of the century, psychologist **G. Stanley Hall** characterized adolescence as a time of **storm and stress**. Current research suggests that most adolescents make it through this time without any more turmoil than they are likely to encounter at other points in their lives.

Cognitive Skills: Cognitively, adolescents begin entering **Piaget's stage of formal operations**. **Adolescent egocentrism** may occur whereby adolescents believe that others are as preoccupied with them as they are with themselves.

1.8 Adulthood

Certain events mark adult attainment in our society. Such events include leaving one's family, supporting oneself, getting married, and having children. Many of these transitions into adulthood involve changes in family relationships and responsibilities.

1.8.1 Early Adulthood

Early adulthood extends from approximately 20 to 40 years of age.

Physical Changes: Reaction time and muscular strength peak in the early to mid-twenties. External signs of aging begin to show in the 30s when the skin loses elasticity and hair becomes thinner and begins to turn gray.

A gain in weight is common because a lowered metabolic rate contributes to increased body fat relative to muscle.

Social Concerns: Social development during early adulthood is focused on forming intimate relationships. Individuals are in Erikson's **intimacy versus isolation** stage.

Cognitive Skills: Intellectual abilities and speed of information processing are relatively stable and gains in intellectual skills are possible during early adulthood. Some studies have shown that approximately 50% of all adults have reached Piaget's stage of **formal operations**.

1.8.2 Middle Adulthood

Middle adulthood lasts from approximately 40 to 65 years of age.

Physical Changes: During middle adulthood the number of active brain cells declines, but the significance of this loss is unclear. In vision, farsightedness increases. Sensitivity to high-frequency sounds decreases. In women, **menopause** (ending of monthly menstruation) occurs at around 51 years of age. The **male climacteric** includes decreased fertility and decreased frequency of orgasm. For both sexes, sexual activity declines although capacity for arousal changes only slightly.

Social Concerns: Over time, individuals become more aware of their own mortality and the passage of time and enter Erikson's **generativity versus stagnation** stage. Those in middle adulthood are often caught between the needs of their children and those of their own aging parents and are thus referred to as the **sandwich generation**.

There has been much debate concerning whether or not most people go through a **midlife crisis**. Many studies have failed to find increased emotional turbulence at midlife.

Cognitive Skills: Effectiveness of retrieval from long-term memory begins a slow decline but is often not noticeable until after age 55. Despite a decreased speed in cognitive processing, intelligence and problem-solving skills usually remain stable. Career development peaks.

1.9 Aging

Gerontologists study aging.

Ageism refers to prejudice against older people.

Physical Changes: **Biological aging** is a gradual process that begins quite early in life. Peak physical functioning occurs around 25 years of age and gradually declines thereafter. The rate of aging is highly individualized. The sensitivity of vision, hearing, and taste decreases in the elderly (those aged 65 and older). Height and weight decreases are also common. The risk of chronic diseases (heart disease, stroke, cancer, etc.) increases. Slower reaction times are common.

Social Concerns: **Elderly adults** are in **Erikson's stage of ego integrity versus despair** and accordingly will be engaged in a **life review**.

Cognitive Skills: A **terminal decline** in intellectual performance occurs in the two to three years that precede an elderly adult's death. **Senile dementia** is an abnormal deterioration in cognitive abilities. **Alzheimer's disease** is a form of dementia.

CHAPTER 2

Personality

2.1 Psychodynamic Approach

Personality refers to distinctive, enduring characteristics or patterns of behavior. An individual's personality reveals itself through consistent behavior in a variety of situations.

This chapter describes different theories that have attempted to explain personality and its development.

Psychodynamic theories (also called **psychoanalytic theories**) of personality descended from **Sigmund Freud** and his theory of personality.

For most psychodynamic theorists, personality is mainly **unconscious**. That is, it is beyond our awareness. In order to understand someone's personality, the **symbolic** meanings of behavior and deep inner workings of the mind must be investigated. Early experiences with parents shape personalities, according to psychodynamic theorists.

2.1.1 Freud's Theory

Sigmund Freud (1856–1939) was a medical doctor from Vienna, Austria, who specialized in neurology. His psychodynamic approach to personality developed as a result of his work with adult patients who had psychiatric and emotional problems.

Freud's theory emphasized three main points:

1. Childhood experiences determine adult personality.

2. Unconscious mental processes influence everyday behavior.

3. Conflict causes most human behavior.

According to Freud, each adult personality consists of an **id**, **ego**, and **superego**.

Personality component	When it develops	How it functions
Id	at birth	Pleasure principle. Unconscious instincts. Irrational. Seeks instant gratification. Contains the libido.
Ego	around 6 months	Reality principle. Mediates id and reality. Executive branch.
Superego	around 6 years	Morality principle. Personal conscience. Personal ideals.

According to Freud, the **id** is unconscious and has no contact with reality. It works according to the **pleasure principle**—the id always seeks pleasure and avoids pain. The id contains the **libido** or sexual energy.

The **ego** evolves from the id and deals with the demands of reality. It is called the **executive branch** of personality because it makes rational decisions. The **reality principle** describes how the ego tries to bring individual id demands within the norms of society. The ego, however, cannot determine if something is right or wrong.

The **superego** is capable of determining if something is right or wrong because it is our conscience. The superego does not consider reality, only rules about moral behavior.

According to Freud, behavior is the outcome of an ongoing series of conflicts between the id, ego, and superego. Conflicts dealing with sexual and aggressive impulses are likely to have far-reaching consequences because social norms dictate that these impulses be routinely frustrated.

Freud considered personality to be like an **iceberg**—most of our personality exists below the level of awareness just as most of an iceberg is hidden beneath the surface of the water. Freud referred to the hidden part of our personality as the **unconscious**. Even though Freud felt that many thoughts, memories, and desires were unconscious, they nonetheless influence our behavior.

The **conscious** part of our personality consists of whatever we are aware of at any particular point in time.

The **preconscious**, according to Freud, contains material that is just below the surface of awareness but can be easily retrieved. An example of preconscious awareness would be your mother's birthdate. You were not thinking of your mother's birthdate but can if you need or want to.

Figure 2.1 presents the iceberg analogy of Freud's notions of unconscious, conscious, and preconscious and how they relate to the three structures of personality (id, ego, and superego).

Defense mechanisms are unconscious methods used by the ego to distort reality and thereby protect us from anxiety. Anxiety can result from the irrational, pleasure demands of the id or from the superego causing guilty feelings about a real or imagined transgression.

Common defense mechanisms are:

Rationalization	Creating false but plausible excuses to justify unacceptable behavior. Example: Reducing guilt for cheating on your taxes by rationalizing "everyone does it."
Repression	Pushing unacceptable id impulses out of awareness and back into the unconscious. Sometimes called "motivated forgetting." Example: Having no memory of an unpleasant experience.
Reaction Formation	Behaving in exactly the opposite of one's true feelings. Example: A mother who feels resentment toward a child may be overly cautious and protective.

Freud's Model of Personality

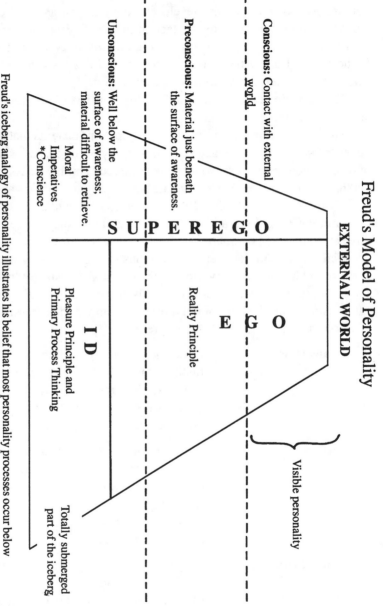

EXTERNAL WORLD

Conscious: Contact with external world.

Preconscious: Material just beneath the surface of awareness.

Unconscious: Well below the surface of awareness; material difficult to retrieve.

SUPEREGO

Moral
Imperatives
*Conscience

Reality Principle

EGO

ID

Pleasure Principle and
Primary Process Thinking

Visible personality

Totally submerged
part of the iceberg

Freud's iceberg analogy of personality illustrates his belief that most personality processes occur below the level of conscious awareness.

Figure 2.1

Regression	Reversion to immature patterns of behavior. Example: Temper tantrums.
Projection	Attributing one's own thoughts, feelings, motives, shortcomings, etc. to others. Example: A wife who constantly suspects her husband of having an affair because unconsciously she has thought of having an affair.
Displacement	Shifting unacceptable feelings from their original source to a safer, substitute target. Example: You are mad at your boss, but you do not yell at your boss; instead you become angry with a family member when you return home.
Sublimation	A useful, socially acceptable course of behavior replaces a socially unacceptable or distasteful impulse. Example: A person who feels aggression due to a lack of control plays an aggressive game of basketball with friends every other day.
Intellectualization	By dealing with a stressful situation in an intellectual and unemotional manner, a person detaches himself from the stress. Example: A person who has lost a family member due to illness will willingly speak of the medical terminology of the illness but will not discuss the emotional aspects of the illness.
Denial	Denying that a very unpleasant thing has happened.

Example: A person with severe stomach pains, possibly an ulcer, refuses to see a doctor because he feels it is only indigestion.

2.1.2 Stages of Psychosexual Development

Freud believed that we go through five stages of psychosexual development in forming our personalities. Each stage represents a different **erogenous zone** or part of the body where pleasure originates.

Freud's Psychosexual Stages

Stage	Age	Erogenous Zone	Description
Oral	0 – 18 months	Mouth	Stimulation of mouth produces pleasure; enjoys sucking, biting, chewing. Weaning is major task or conflict.
Anal	18 – 36 months	Anus	Toilet training is major task. Expelling and retaining feces produces pleasure.
Phallic	3 – 6 years	Genitals	Self-stimulation of genitals produces pleasure. **Oedipal** (for boys) and **Electra** (for girls) conflicts occur—children have erotic desires for opposite-sex parent as well as feelings of fear and hostility for same-sex parent. Successful resolution of this conflict results in identification with same-sex parent.

Stage	Age	Erogenous Zone	Description
Latency	6 – 12 years	None	Sexual feelings are repressed. Social contacts beyond immediate family are expanded.
Genital	Puberty onward	Genitals	Establishing intimate, sexual relations with others is main focus.

According to Freud, children experience conflicts between urges in their erogenous zones and societal rules. **Fixation** can result when these urges are either frustrated or overindulged in any one erogenous zone. Fixation results in one's personality becoming permanently locked in the conflict surrounding that erogenous zone.

Freud felt that the first three psychosexual stages were the most important for personality development. Examples of possible personality traits resulting from fixations in the first three psychosexual stages are presented here.

Stage	Examples of traits related to fixation
Oral	Obsessive eating Smoking Drinking Sarcasm Overly demanding Aggressiveness
Anal	Extreme messiness Overly orderly Overly concerned about punctuality Fear of dirt Love of bathroom humor Anxiety about sexual activities Overly giving Rebelliousness

Phallic	Excessive masturbation
	Flirts frequently
	Excessive modesty
	Excessively timid
	Overly proud
	Promiscuity

2.1.3 Neo-Freudians

Neo-Freudians are personality theorists who started their careers as followers of Freud but eventually disagreed on some of the basic principles of his theory.

Theorists include Carl Jung, Alfred Adler, and Karen Horney. They disagreed with the importance Freud placed on psychosexual development and the importance of childhood experiences on personality development. Though they believed childhood experiences do play a role in development, future goals in middle age are more important for personality development.

2.1.4 Evaluating the Psychodynamic Approach

Freud and neo-Freudians have contributed to our understanding of personality and personality development:

- They suggested that early experiences can shape our personality and that personality can best be understood by examining it developmentally.

- Freud encouraged psychologists to study human emotions and motivation.

- The concept of the unconscious is still valuable to many psychologists.

- They developed psychotherapies based on their theories. (See chapter 6.)

Criticisms of the psychodynamic approach include:

It is untestable. For example, ideas such as the unconscious are difficult to measure.

Data to support these theories often come from case studies of individual clients or from clients' memories. Memories may be flawed and therapists may see what they expect to see based on their theoretical orientation.

Freud's theory is pessimistic about human nature.

Freud's theory is sexist and biased against women.

2.2 Behavioral Perspective

The **behaviorist perspective** is that personality is a collection of **learned behavior patterns**. Personality, like any other learned behavior, is acquired through classical and operant conditioning, social learning, discrimination, and generalization.

2.2.1 Skinner's Ideas

B. F. Skinner (1904 – 1990) and other traditional behaviorists believed that everything a person does is ultimately based on past and present rewards and punishments and other aspects of operant conditioning. He rejected the idea that personality is made up of consistent traits and denied that a personality or self initiates or directs behavior.

Skinner did not use the term personality. For Skinner, what other theorists call personality is nothing more than a collection of learned behaviors that have been reinforced in the past.

For Skinner, therefore, personality is a person's observed behaviors and does not contain internal traits or thoughts. Consistency in behavior occurs because of consistency in environmental experiences. Also, according to behaviorists, because personality is learned, it can be changed by rearranging experiences and situations.

2.2.2 Social Learning

The group of psychologists who emphasize behavior, environment, and cognition as important in determining personality are known as **social learning theorists** (sometimes referred to as **cognitive-behavioral** or **social-cognitive approach**).

Social learning theorists differ from the behavioral view of Skinner by emphasizing that we can regulate and control our own behavior despite changes in our environment.

Albert Bandura, Walter Mischel, and **Julian Rotter** are three social learning theorists.

Bandura believes that learning occurs by observing what others do and that these observations form an important part of our personality. Bandura suggested that how people behave in a variety of situations is determined by **self-efficacy** or their expectations of success. Those high in self-efficacy will approach new situations confidently and persist in their efforts because they believe success is likely. People low in self-efficacy expect to do poorly and avoid challenges.

According to Bandura, **reciprocal determinism** (sometimes called **reciprocal influences**) influences individual differences in personality. This means that personality, behavior, and environment constantly influence one another and shape each other in a reciprocal fashion.

According to **Mischel,** person variables as well as situation variables are important in explaining behavior. Mischel believes that behavior is characterized more by **situational specificity** than by consistency. That is, we often behave differently in different situations.

Rotter believed personality is determined by a person's **generalized expectations** about future outcomes and reinforcements. Rotter proposed that **locus of control** influences how we behave. Those with an **internal locus of control** see themselves primarily in control of their behavior and its consequences. Persons with an **external locus of control** see their behavior as controlled by fate, chance, or luck and are less likely to change their behavior as a result of reinforcement because they do not understand the relationship between the reinforcement and their behavior.

2.2.3 Evaluating the Behavioral Perspective

The main strengths of the behavior perspective are its strong research base and testability.

Criticisms of the behavioral perspective of personality include:

They do not consider possible unconscious motives or internal dispositions or traits that might be consistent from situation to situation.

There has been little effort to integrate possible biological factors or genetic influences into their theories of personality.

Historically, they have relied too much on animal research.

They have not paid attention to possible enduring qualities of personality.

They tend to be **reductionistic,** meaning they try to explain the complex concept of personality in terms of one or two factors.

They have focused more on environment and less on cognition.

2.3 The Trait Approach

The **trait** or **dispositional approaches** to personality focus on durable tendencies or dispositions to behave in a particular way in a variety of situations. According to trait theories, people can be described in terms of the basic ways that they behave, such as friendly, moody, dependable, etc.

While trait theorists sometimes disagree on which traits make up personality, they all agree that traits are the fundamental building blocks of personality. Trait theorists also debate how many dimensions are necessary to describe personality. Most trait approaches assume that some traits are more basic than others.

Basic assumptions of the trait approach to personality are:

1. Each person has **stable dispositions** to display certain behaviors, attitudes, and emotions.

2. These dispositions or traits are **general** and appear in **diverse situations**.

3. Each person has a **different set of traits**.

4. Trait theorists include Gordon Allport, Hans Eysenck, and Raymond Cattell.

2.3.1 Basic Five Traits

More recently, a number of studies have revealed five basic dimensions of personality. These are referred to as the **Big Five traits** or **factors** of personality.

There has been some disagreement about how to name these five traits. Three possible listings include:

extraversion-introversion
friendly compliance versus hostile noncompliance
neuroticism
will to achieve
intellect

or

extraversion
agreeableness
conscientiousness
emotional stability
openness to experience

or

extraversion
neuroticism
agreeableness
openness to experience
conscientiousness

2.3.2 Sheldon's Body Types

An American physician, **William Sheldon,** found a moderate correlation between body type or physique and personality.

Body type (physique)		Personality
Endomorph	⟶	**Viscerotonic**
Soft, round, fairly weak muscles and bones		Relaxed, loves to eat, sociable
Mesomorph	⟶	**Somatotonic**
Muscular, athletic		Energetic, assertive, courageous

Ectomorph ⟶	Cerebrotonic
Thin, physically weak, sensitive nervous system	Restrained, fearful, introvert, artistic

There is no research evidence, however, to validate the relationship between body type and personality, and Sheldon's theory is not popular today.

2.3.3 Evaluating the Trait Approach

There is evidence to support the view that there are internal traits that strongly influence behavior across situations and some traits appear stable over time.

Criticisms of the trait theory maintain:

Personality often does change according to a given situation.

Trait theorists do not attempt to explain why people have certain traits and it is, therefore, not a comprehensive approach to the study of personality.

Trait approach is more of a research technique than a theory.

The debate continues concerning what (and how many) traits are related to personality.

2.4 The Humanistic Approach

The **humanistic approach** (sometimes referred to as **phenomenological approach**) to personality is an **optimistic** response to the pessimism of psychodynamic theorists. Humanistic psychologists emphasize immediate **subjective experiences** that are unique to each of us.

The humanistic approach stresses each person's capacity for personal growth, positive growth, free will, and freedom to choose one's destiny.

2.4.1 Rogers' Person-Centered Approach

Carl Rogers' (1902–1987) **person-centered approach** emphasizes that people have different perceived realities, strive toward self-actualization, and should be given unconditional positive regard.

Rogers used the term **phenomenal field** to describe each person's total subjective experience of reality.

The **self-concept** (or **self-image**) is the core theme in Rogers' theory. Self-concept refers to individuals, overall perceptions of their abilities, behavior, and personality. He distinguished between the **real self** (the self we form as a result of our experiences) and the **ideal self** (who we really want to be).

Maladjustment results from a discrepancy between the real self and the ideal self. An **incongruent person** is one who has a distorted or inaccurate self-image.

Experiences that match the self-image are **symbolized** and admitted to consciousness.

The development of the self-concept depends on **self-evaluations** and **positive evaluations** shown by **others**. Anxiety and other problems result, therefore, because of **incongruence** between self-evaluations and the evaluations of others.

Others can help a person develop a more positive self-concept through **unconditional positive regard**. That is, by being accepting, positive, and loving without special conditions or strings attached and regardless of the person's behavior.

Rogers also felt we can help others develop their self-concept by being **empathetic** (sensitive and understanding) and **genuine** (open with our feelings and dropping our pretenses).

According to Rogers, **fully functioning persons** are those who live in harmony with their deepest feelings, impulses, and intuitions. Rogers used the term **self-actualization** to describe the tendency for humans to fulfill their true potential.

(Psychotherapy based on Rogers' theory is presented in chapter 6.)

2.4.2 Maslow's Theory of Self-Actualization

Abraham Maslow (1908–1970) is another humanistic psychologist and is best known for his study of **self-actualization**. Maslow studied individuals who he believed were using their abilities to their full potential. He found that these self-actualizers were accurate in perceiving reality, comfortable with life, accepting of themselves and others, did not depend on external authority, were autonomous and independent, had a good sense of humor about themselves and others, and had frequent **peak experiences** (experiences of insight and deep meaning).

Maslow developed a **hierarchy of motives** or **hierarchy of needs** in which each lower need must be satisfied before the next level can be addressed. These needs occur in the following sequence: **physiological, safety, love and belongingness, esteem,** and finally, **self-actualization.** (Maslow's hierarchy of motives is described in further detail in chapter 4).

2.4.3 Evaluating the Humanistic Approach

The humanistic or phenomenological approach has been useful in developing several types of psychotherapy and in suggesting child-rearing and educational practices. Other strengths are its positive interpretation of human nature and its focus on the present and future.

Criticisms of the humanistic or phenomenological approach include:

This approach may be better at describing behavior than explaining behavior.

The studies to support this approach are often inadequate and unscientific.

It is too selfish in focus. Humanistic theorists focus on what is good for the self but often ignore what is good for the general welfare of others.

It is too optimistic. The belief that all humans are driven by a positive and innate growth potential may be naive and unrealistic.

CHAPTER 3

Assessing Intelligence and Personality

3.1 Developing Tests

Assessing intelligence and personality is a complex activity. **Assessment**, in general, is an information-gathering process that leads to decisions concerning classification, placement, and treatment. Tests, observations, and interviews are the most common procedures used in the assessment process. This chapter focuses on tests used to determine intelligence and personality.

A **psychological test** is an objective, standardized measure of a sample of behavior. Both intelligence and personality tests are considered psychological tests.

Any good psychological test must meet three criteria—it must be standardized, reliable, and valid.

3.1.1 Standardization

Standardization involves developing uniform procedures for administering and scoring a test, and developing norms for the test.

Uniform procedures require that the testing environment, test directions, test items, and amount of time allowed be as similar as possible for all individuals who take the test.

Norms are established standards of performance for a test. Norms inform us about which scores are considered high, average, or low. Norms are determined by giving the test to a large group of people **representative** of the **population** for whom the test is intended. Future test-takers' scores are determined by comparing their scores with those from the **standardization sample** or group that determined the norms.

A **percentile score** indicates the percentage of people who scored below a score that one has attained. If you attain a percentile score of 75, for example, that means that you scored higher than 75% of the sample of people who provided the test norms.

3.1.2 Reliability

Reliability is a measure of the consistency of a person's test scores. A test's reliability can be measured in several ways:

Test-retest reliability	Giving the same individuals the same test on two different occasions. If the results are similar, then the test is considered to have good test-retest reliability.
Split-half reliability	Individuals take only one test, but the test items are divided into two halves and performance on each half is compared. If individuals performed about equally well on each half of the test, the test has good split-half reliability.
Alternate-form reliability	Two alternate forms of the test are administered on two different occasions. Test items on the two forms are similar but not identical. If each person's score is similar on the two tests, alternate-form reliability is high.

Correlation coefficients are usually used to represent reliability. A correlation coefficient is a numerical index that represents the degree of relationship between two variables.

3.1.3 Validity

A valid test is one that measures what it purports to measure. Methods to measure validity include:

Content validity	The test's ability to cover the complete range of material (or content) that it is supposed to measure.
Criterion validity	Compares test scores to actual performance on another direct and independent measure of what the test is supposed to measure.
Predictive validity	A form of criterion validity. How well a test score predicts an individual's performance at some time in the future.
Face validity	How well the test and test items appear to be relevant.
Construct validity	How well a test appears to represent a **theoretical or hypothetical construct** (abstract qualities). It is the extent to which scores on a test behave in accordance with a theory about the construct of interest.

3.2 Intelligence Testing

Aptitude tests attempt to measure a person's capability for mastering an area of knowledge. (For instance, what is your potential or aptitude for learning a foreign language?)

Achievement tests assess the amount of knowledge someone has already acquired in a specific area (such as math achievement, reading achievement, etc.).

Because intelligence is a **hypothetical construct**, psychologists have disagreed on how to define it. Different intelligence tests, therefore, ask different questions and may measure different abilities.

Some definitions of intelligence include:

- The capacity to acquire and use knowledge.
- The total body of acquired knowledge.
- The ability to arrive at innovative solutions to problems.
- The ability to deal effectively with one's environment.
- Knowledge of one's culture.
- The ability to do well in school.
- It is the global capacity of the individual to act purposefully, to think rationally, and to deal effectively with the environment.
- Intelligence is what intelligence tests measure.

A major question related to intelligence has been "does intelligence consist of a single core factor or does it consist of many separate, unrelated abilities?" Responses to this include:

Charles Spearman	Concluded that cognitive abilities could be narrowed down to one critical **g-factor** or general intelligence. (The **s-factors** represent specific knowledge needed to answer questions on a particular test.)
J. P. Guilford	Proposed that intelligence consists of 150 distinct abilities.
L. L. Thurstone	Used a statistical technique known as **factor analysis** to find seven independent primary mental abilities: numerical ability, reasoning, verbal fluency, spatial visualization, perceptual ability, memory, and verbal comprehension.
Raymond B. Cattell	Argued that a g-factor does exist, but it consists of **fluid intelligence**

	(reasoning and problem solving) and **crystallized intelligence** (specific knowledge gained from applying fluid intelligence).
Robert Sternberg	Proposed a **triarchic theory of intelligence** that specifies three important parts of intelligence: **componential intelligence** (includes metacomponents, performance components, and knowledge-acquisition components), **experiential intelligence** (abilities to deal with novelty and to automatize processing), and **contextual intelligence** (practical intelligence and social intelligence).
Howard Gardner	**Theory of multiple intelligences** proposed seven different components of intelligence that include not only language ability, logical-mathematical thinking, and spatial thinking but also musical, bodily kinesthetic, interpersonal, and intrapersonal thinking.

3.2.1 History of Intelligence Testing

Early interest in intelligence testing dates back to the **eugenics movement** of **Sir Frances Galton**. Galton believed that it is possible to improve genetic characteristics (including intelligence) through breeding.

The first effective test of intelligence was devised in the early 1900s by French psychologist **Alfred Binet**. Binet was appointed by the French Ministry of Public Instruction to design an intelligence test that would identify children who needed to be removed from the regular classrooms so that they could receive special instruction.

Binet and his colleague **Theodore Simon** devised an intelligence test consisting of 30 subtests containing problems of increasing difficulty. The items on the test were designed to measure children's judgment, reasoning, and comprehension. This first test was published in 1905 and then revised in 1908 and 1911.

The 1908 revision of the Binet and Simon scale introduced the notion of **mental age**. Mental age is a measure of a child's intellectual level that is independent of the child's **chronological age** (actual age).

Shortly after Binet's original work, **Lewis M. Terman** of Stanford University and his colleagues helped refine and standardize the test for American children. Their version came to be the **Stanford-Binet Intelligence Scale**, and its latest revision is still being used today. (A further discussion of this scale can be found later in this chapter.)

Terman and others (e.g., **L. William Stern** of Germany) developed the idea of the **IQ** or **intelligence quotient** (sometimes referred to as **ratio IQ score**).

To **calculate IQ**, a child's **mental age (MA)** (as determined by how well she/he does on the test) is **divided by** her/his **chronological age (CA)** and **multiplied by 100**. That is,

$$IQ = \frac{MA}{CA} \times 100$$

The major advantage of the IQ score over simple MA is that it gives an index of a child's IQ test performance relative to others of the same chronological age.

The major problem with the ratio IQ score is that most people's mental development slows in their late teens. But as MA may remain fairly stable throughout adulthood, CA increases over time. Using CA as the divisor in the IQ formula, therefore, results in an individual's IQ score diminishing over time (even though MA has not changed).

David Wechsler corrected this problem with ratio IQ scores by devising the **deviation IQ score**. This deviation IQ score is calculated by converting the raw scores on each subtest of the test to **standard scores** normalized for each age group. These standard scores are then translated into deviation IQ scores.

Wechsler reasoned that intelligence is **normally distributed** or follows the bell-shaped curve—that is, the majority of people score at or around the **mean** or average score of 100 and progressively fewer people will achieve scores that spread out in either direction of the mean. A group of IQ scores can be portrayed as a normal, bell-shaped curve with an average score of 100 and a **standard deviation** (average deviation from the mean) that is the same (i.e., 15) at every age level. Figure 3.2 presents the normal distribution of intelligence scores.

The advantage of the deviation IQ is that the standing of an individual can be compared with the scores of others of the same age, and the intervals from age to age remain the same. **Deviation IQ scores**, therefore, indicate exactly where a test-taker falls in the normal distribution of intelligence.

Terman adopted the deviation IQ as the scoring standard for the 1960 revision of the Stanford-Binet Intelligence Scale, although he chose a standard deviation of 16 rather than 15. Almost all other intelligence tests today use deviation IQ scores.

3.2.2 Current Intelligence Tests

The two most widely used versions of intelligence tests today are described next. These tests are **individually administered**, which means that they are given only by trained psychologists to one test-taker at a time.

The first **Stanford-Binet Intelligence Scale** was published in 1916 by **Lewis Terman** and his colleagues. It was revised in 1937, 1960, 1986 and 2003 and remains one of the world's most widely used tests of intelligence (although there are criticisms of the scale). It can be used with individuals from age two through adulthood.

In the 1986 revision, Stanford-Binet Intelligence Scale: Fourth Edition, the term intelligence was replaced by cognitive development. The terms intelligence, IQ, and mental age are no longer used; instead the term **Standard Age Score (SAS)** is used. The current edition measures five areas of cognitive development and a SAS can be calculated for each area as well as an overall composite score. The five areas measured are called Fluid Reasoning, Knowledge, Quantitative Reasoning, Visual-Spatial Processing, and Working Memory.

Because the Stanford-Binet initially appeared to be unsatisfactory for use with adults, in 1939 David Wechsler published a test

Normal Distribution of Intelligence
(Based on tests with a standard deviation of 15)

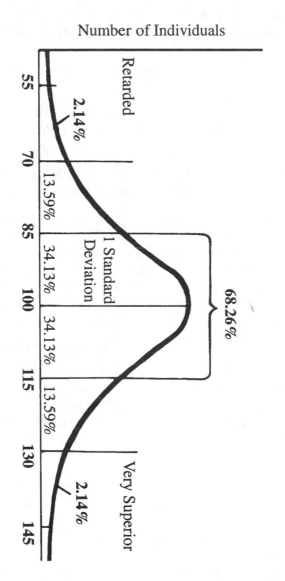

Number of Individuals

Retarded

2.14%

55 70 85 100 115 130 145

13.59% | 34.13% | 34.13% | 13.59%

1 Standard Deviation

68.26%

Very Superior

2.14%

IQ SCORES

Approximately two-thirds of the IQ scores of any age group fall within one standard deviation above and below the mean score of 100. Notice that extremely high and extremely low scores are rare.

Figure 3.2

45

designed exclusively for adults. This test has since been revised and is now known at the **WAIS-R** or **Wechsler Adult Intelligence Scale, Revised**.

Eventually, Wechsler published two scales for children and these are now known as:

WPPSI-R   **Wechsler Preschool and Primary Scale of Intelligence, Revised** (for children 4 to 6 years of age)

WISC-III   **Wechsler Intelligence Scale for Children, 3rd edition** (for children 6 to 16 years of age)

The Wechsler scales were known for at least two major innovations when they were first developed. First, they were less dependent on verbal ability than the Stanford-Binet and included many items that required nonverbal reasoning. His tests allow the computation of three scores, a **Verbal IQ score**, a **Performance IQ score**, and an overall **Full Scale IQ score**. For example, subtests from the verbal and performance sections of the **WAIS-R** include:

Verbal Subtests	Performance Subtests
Information	Digit Symbol
Comprehension	Picture Completion
Arithmetic	Block Design
Similarities	Picture Arrangement
Digit Span	Object Assembly
Vocabulary	

Second, Wechsler developed the **deviation IQ score** based on the normal distribution of intelligence and abandoned the notion of intelligence quotient.

Wechsler's scales of intelligence are still widely used and respected today.

Intelligence tests, as with any other test, must fit certain requirements in order to be of good quality.

Reliability. Most intelligence tests used today (e.g., Stanford-Binet and Wechsler scales) demonstrate good reliability or consistency of scores.

Validity. The validity of intelligence tests depends on the criterion being used. For example, they do a good job of predicting success in school. Although intelligence test scores correlate with occupational attainment, they do not predict performance within a given occupation.

Stability. Intelligence test scores can and do change over time. For instance, infant and preschool scores are not good predictors of intelligence in later childhood, adolescence, or adulthood. It is not until late elementary school (e.g., after age 8 – 10) that intelligence test scores begin to stabilize. It is also possible, however, to make substantial gains or losses in intelligence during adolescence and adulthood.

3.2.3 Extremes of Intelligence

Two basic extremes of intellectual performance are demonstrated on the extreme left and right of the normal distribution (see figure 3.1) for intelligence.

In order to be considered **mentally retarded**, an individual must meet all three of the essential features described below:

1. Intellectual functioning must be **significantly below average**. Today intelligence test scores of below 70—or 2 standard deviations below the mean—are considered significantly below average.

2. Significant deficits in **adaptive functioning** must be evident. Adaptive functioning refers to social competence or independent behavior that is expected based on chronological age.

3. Onset must be **prior** to **age 18**.

Four general categories or ways of classifying mental retardation include:

Category	Percentage	IQ Range	Characteristics
Mild	80%	50 – 70	May complete 6th grade academic work; may learn vocational skills and hold a job; may live independently as an adult.

Category	Percentage	IQ Range	Characteristics
Moderate	12%	35 – 49	May complete 2nd grade academic work; can learn social and occupational skills; may hold job in sheltered workshop.
Severe	7%	20 – 34	May learn to talk or communicate; through repetition may learn basic health habits; often needs help for simple tasks.
Profound	1%	less than 20	Little or no speech; may learn limited self-help skills; requires constant help and supervision.

There are hundreds of known causes of mental retardation. Many of them are biological, genetic, chromosomal, prenatal, perinatal, and postnatal in origin. Mental retardation can also result from environmental influences such as sensory or maternal deprivation. In some cases (especially mild mental retardation), the cause of an individual child's mental retardation is unknown.

Giftedness is often defined as having an intelligence of 120 to 130 or higher (or having an IQ in the upper 2 to 3 percent of the population).

Lewis Terman began a **longitudinal study** of gifted children in the 1920s. That is, he and others followed the lives of these children as they grew up and became adults. The study will not be completed until the year 2010. The average intelligence score was 150 for the approximately 1,500 children in this study. The findings of this study have challenged the commonly held belief that the intellectually gifted are emotionally disturbed and socially maladjusted. In fact, just the opposite was found. As adults, this group was also more academically and professionally successful than their non-gifted peers.

Creativity is the ability to think about something in novel and unusual ways and to come up with unique solutions to problems.

Creativity usually involves **divergent thinking** or the ability to generate many different but plausible responses to a problem. Creative individuals tend to be more independent, rely more on intuitive thinking, have a higher degree of self-acceptance, and have more energy. Personality disorders are not more common among creative individuals.

There is not a very high correlation between intelligence and creativity. This is because most intelligence tests measure **convergent thinking** (producing one correct answer) and do not measure divergent thinking.

3.2.4 Determinants of Intelligence

The **nature vs. nurture debate** related to intelligence addresses whether heredity or environment determines one's intellectual skills.

Heritability is an estimate of how much of a trait in a population is determined by genetic inheritance.

In the late 1960s, **Arthur Jensen** argued that intelligence is approximately 80% due to heredity. He felt that the difference in mean intelligence scores for different races, nationalities, and social classes was due more to heredity than to environment.

Correlational studies with twins suggest that heredity influences the development of intelligence. For instance, the correlation of intelligence test scores for identical twins (who have identical genetic make-up) is higher than the correlation for fraternal twins. Even identical twins reared apart have more similar IQs than fraternal twins reared together in the same household.

There is research evidence, however, to indicate that environment also exerts a strong influence on intelligence. **Sandra Scarr** and other researchers have shown that underprivileged children placed in homes that provide an enriching intellectual environment have shown moderate but consistent increases in intelligence. Children placed in various enrichment programs have also shown gains in IQ. The IQs of identical twins reared together in the same environment are more similar than those for identical twins reared apart.

The term **reaction range** has been applied to the nature vs. nurture debate of intelligence. **Reaction range** implies that genetics may limit or define a potential range of IQ but that environment can influence where along this range an individual's IQ score falls. For instance, children in an enriched environment should score near the top of their potential IQ range.

Racial and cultural differences in IQ are very small when compared to the range of genetic differences within each group. Research has suggested, for example, that the differences between mean intelligence test scores for black and white Americans may be due to differences in parental education, nutrition, health care, schools, and motivation for doing well on the test.

Many have argued that intelligence tests are **culturally biased** because they have been developed by white, middle-class psychologists. There is some research evidence to support this claim. Attempts have been made to produce language-free, culture-fair tests of intelligence. The **Raven's Progressive Matrices** is one such test.

3.3 Personality Testing

Psychologists use **personality tests** for four different purposes:

1. to aid in the diagnosis of psychological disorders,
2. to counsel people,
3. to select employees,
4. to conduct research.

There are three major categories of personality tests: self-report inventories, projector tests, and behavioral assessment.

3.3.1 Self-Report Inventories

Self-report inventories instruct people to answer questions about themselves—about their characteristic behaviors, beliefs, and feelings.

The most widely used self-report inventory is the **MMPI** or **Minnesota Multiphasic Personality Inventory**. The MMPI was recently revised and is now known as the **MMPI-2**.

The MMPI was originally designed to aid in the diagnosis of psychological disorders. It measures aspects of personality that, when manifested to an extreme degree, are thought to be symptoms of disorders.

The MMPI-2 consists of 567 statements that require a "true,"
"false," or "cannot say" response. Sample statements include:
"People are out to get me."
"I smile at everyone I meet."
"I know who is responsible for my troubles."
The MMPI yields scores on 14 subscales—4 validity scales and
10 clinical scales.

The **validity scales** are used to determine if an individual has
been careless or deceptive in taking the test. The validity scales
include:

Cannot say scale
Lie scale
Infrequency scale
Subtle defensiveness scale

The **clinical scales** measure various aspects of personality and
include:

Hypocondriasis scale
Depression scale
Hysteria scale
Psychopathic deviation scale
Masculinity/femininity scale
Paranoia scale
Psychasthenia scale
Schizophrenia scale
Hypomania scale
Social introversion scale

Although most of the original items were kept, the MMPI-2
resulted in a deletion of some statements from the original version.
For instance, all items pertaining to religion and most of the questions about sexual practices were deleted. Other statements were
reworded to update obsolete language, to make them more under-
standable, and to correct sexist language. Although the basic clinical scales were not changed, **content scales** that relate to substance
abuse, eating disorders, Type-A behavior, repression, anger, cyni-
cism, low self-esteem, family problems, and inability to function
in a job were added.

The MMPI can be scored by computer. A high score on any one of the scales does not necessarily mean that a person has a problem or psychological disorder. People with most types of disorders show elevated scores on several MMPI scales. Psychologists look at patterns of scores to determine problem areas. Thus, the interpretation of MMPI scores is quite complicated.

Research has shown that the MMPI is a reliable test that is easy to administer and score and is inexpensive to use.

Although the MMPI is the most popular and widely used personality test for diagnosing psychological problems (it has been translated into 115 languages), it is not without its critics. For instance, the MMPI does not reveal differences among normal personalities very well. As mentioned previously, interpretation of results is a complex process.

3.3.2 Projective Testing

Projective tests are personality tests that present an ambiguous stimulus that subjects are asked to describe or explain. The assumption is that people respond by projecting their own inner thoughts, feelings, fears, or conflicts into the test materials. Projective tests are designed to elicit unconscious conflicts and feelings and are sometimes referred to as **psychoanalytic tests**.

The two most famous projective tests are the Rorschach Inkblot Test and the Thematic Apperception Test.

Swiss psychiatrist **Hermann Rorschach** developed the **Rorschach Inkblot Test** in 1921.

This test consists of ten inkblots—half in black and white and half in color—that subjects are asked to describe. The examiner then goes through the cards again and asks questions to clarify what the subject has reported.

Five different scoring systems exist for scoring Rorschach responses. Responses can be analyzed in terms of content, whether the subject uses the whole inkblot or just part of it, originality, and the feature of the inkblot that determined the response. The examiner also considers whether the subject saw movement, human figures, animal figures, etc. in the inkblots.

Rorschach Inkblot

Figure 3.3

The Rorschach continues to be widely used in clinical circles. Its advocates feel that the freedom of response encouraged by this test makes it an important clinical tool.

Critics, however, point out that the Rorschach has yet to demonstrate adequate reliability and validity and relies too heavily on interpretations made by the examiner.

Figure 3.3 is an example of an inkblot used in the Rorschach test.

The **Thematic Apperception Test (TAT)** is a projective test that was developed by **Henry Murray** and his colleagues in 1935.

The TAT consists of one blank card and nineteen other cards showing vague or ambiguous black-and-white drawings of human figures in various situations. The examiner chooses ten or fewer cards and presents them one at a time. Subjects are asked to tell a story about each card. As with the Rorschach, it is assumed that a person projects her/his own unconscious thoughts and feelings into their story.

The test's results are analyzed according to Murray's list of needs, which includes the need for achievement, affiliation, and aggression. Responses to each story are scored in terms of heroes, needs, themes, and outcome to provide insight into the subject's personality.

The TAT is time-consuming and difficult to administer. It relies too heavily on the interpretation skills of the examiner and has not demonstrated adequate reliability and validity. It may also reflect a person's temporary motivational state and neglect more permanent aspects of personality.

3.3.3 Behavioral Assessment

Behavioral assessment attempts to obtain more objective information about personality by observing an individual's behavior directly. The assumption is that personality cannot be evaluated apart from the environment.

Behavior assessment is a technique favored by behaviorists.

One method of behavioral assessment is **naturalistic observation,** which is the systematic recording of behavior in the natural environment, usually by trained observers.

Behavioral assessment can also occur outside of a natural setting. For instance, behavior may be assessed in a clinical setting or when a therapist has modified some aspect of the environment and observes its effect on behavior.

CHAPTER 4

Motivation and Emotion

4.1 Motivation

Psychologists study motivation because they want to know why a behavior occurs. Motivation is the process that initiates, directs, and sustains behavior while simultaneously satisfying physiological or psychological needs. A **motive** is a reason or purpose for behavior.

4.1.1 Theories of Motivation

Several theories describe the basis for motivation.

An **instinct** is an inborn, unlearned, fixed pattern of behavior that is biologically determined and is characteristic of an entire species. The idea of attributing human and animal behavior to instincts was not seriously considered until **Charles Darwin** suggested that humans evolved from lower animals.

William McDougall believed that instincts were "the prime movers of all human activity." He identified 18 instincts, including parental instinct, curiosity, escape, reproduction, self-assertion, pugnacity, and gregariousness. However, psychologists do not agree on what and how many human instincts there are. While McDougall suggested 18, others suggested even more.

Instinct theory was widely accepted by psychologists for the first 20 or 30 years of this century. Today, the idea that motivation is based on instincts has been replaced by other theories because psychologists recognized that human behavior is too diverse and unpredictable to be consistent across our species. Further, there is no scientific way to prove the existence of instincts in humans. Many feel that instinct theory provides a description rather than an explanation of behavior.

Drive-reduction theory was popularized by **Clark Hull** and suggests that motivation results from attempting to keep a balanced internal state.

Homeostasis is the built-in tendency to maintain internal stability or equilibrium. Any deviation from homeostasis creates a **need**. A need results in a drive for action. A **drive**, therefore, is a psychological state of tension or arousal that motivates activities to reduce this tension and restore homeostatic balance.

Primary drives are drives that arise from biological needs. **Secondary drives** are learned through operant or classical conditioning.

Drive-reduction theory can be diagrammed as:

Lack of Homeostasis

↓

Need

↓

Drive

↓

Motivation to Act

↓

Homeostasis

For instance, homeostasis works to maintain a constant internal body temperature in humans of approximately 98.6 degrees Fahrenheit. If body temperature goes above this average temperature, our bodies automatically respond (e.g., perspiration) to restore equilibrium. These automatic responses may not be sufficient by themselves, and we may be motivated to take other actions (e.g., remove some clothing).

The nervous systems are involved in maintaining homeostasis. For instance, the **parasympathetic branch** acts to counteract heat and the **sympathetic branch** responds to cold. Both of these branches are governed by the **hypothalamus**, a structure found near the base of the forebrain that is involved in the regulation of basic biological needs (e.g., temperature, hunger, thirst).

Drive theories, however, cannot explain all motivation. Motivation can exist without drive arousal. For instance, we often eat when there is no need to eat (i.e., we are not physically hungry).

Incentive theories propose that external stimuli regulate motivational states (e.g., the sight of a hot fudge sundae motivates eating), and that human behavior is goal-directed. That is, anticipated rewards (i.e., the taste of the sundae) can direct and encourage behavior. Rewards, in motivational terms, are incentives, and behavior is goal-directed to obtain these rewards. Incentives vary from person to person and can change over time.

Many psychologists believe that instead of contradicting each other, drive and incentive theories may work together in motivating behavior.

Arousal theory suggests that the aim of motivation is to maintain an optimal level of arousal. **Arousal** is a person's state of alertness and mental and physical activation. If arousal is less than the optimal level, we do something to stimulate it. If arousal is greater than the optimal level, we seek to reduce the stimulation. The level of arousal considered optimal varies from person to person.

The **Yerkes-Dodson law** states that a particular level of motivational arousal produces optimal performance on a task. Research suggests that people perform best when arousal is moderate. On easy or simple tasks, people can perform better under higher levels of arousal. On difficult or complex tasks, the negative effects of over–arousal are particularly strong.

Richard Solomon proposed an **opponent-process theory** of motivation. This theory argues that one emotional state will trigger an opposite emotional state that lasts long after the original emotion has disappeared. That is, an increase in arousal will produce a calming reaction in the nervous system, and vice versa. It is the opponent

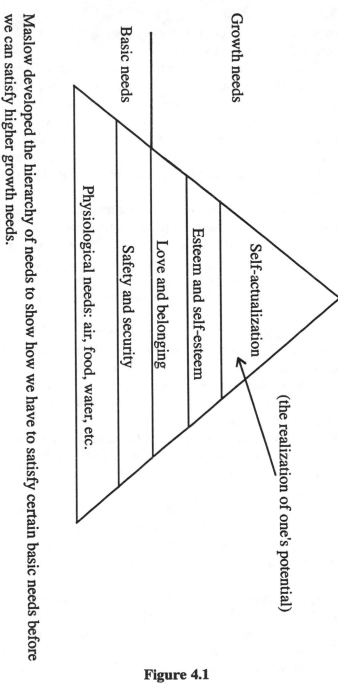

Growth needs

Basic needs

Self-actualization

(the realization of one's potential)

Esteem and self-esteem

Love and belonging

Safety and security

Physiological needs: air, food, water, etc.

Maslow developed the hierarchy of needs to show how we have to satisfy certain basic needs before we can satisfy higher growth needs.

Figure 4.1

59

process, not the initial reaction, therefore, that maintains the motivation to carry out certain behaviors.

For instance, opponent-process theory suggests that the fear that skydivers feel when risking their lives will trigger an extremely positive emotional response. As a consequence, the motivation to skydive increases. This theory has also been used to explain the motivation behind risky, dangerous behaviors as well as drug addiction.

Abraham Maslow, a humanistic theorist, proposed a **hierarchy of needs** to explain motivations. Figure 4.1 presents this hierarchy in its pyramidal form.

According to Maslow, human needs are arranged in a hierarchy. People must satisfy their **basic** or **physiological needs** before they can satisfy their **higher-order needs**. Individuals progress upward in the hierarchy when lower needs are satisfied, but they may regress to lower levels if basic needs are no longer satisfied. As one moves up the hierarchy, each level of needs becomes less biological and more social in origin.

For instance, Maslow proposed that the basic, fundamental needs essential for survival, such as food, water, stable body temperature, etc. must be met first. When a person satisfies a level of physiological needs, this satisfaction activates needs at the next level. This means that after basic **physiological needs** are met, **safety and security needs** become motivating.

Following this pattern, only when the basic physiological and safety needs are met can a person consider fulfilling higher-order needs, consisting of **love and belonging, esteem and self-esteem**, and **self-actualization**.

Love and belonging needs include the need to obtain and give affection and to be a contributing member of society.

Esteem and self-esteem relate to the need to develop a sense of self-worth by knowing that others are aware of one's competence and value.

The highest need in Maslow's motivational hierarchy is the need for **self-actualization**, which is the need to fulfill one's potential. According to Maslow, people will be frustrated if they are unable to fully use their talents or pursue their true interests. A state of self-actualization provides a sense of satisfaction with one's current state of affairs.

Psychologists feel that Maslow's theory is important because it highlights the complexity of human needs. It also emphasizes that basic biological needs must be met before people will be concerned with higher-order needs.

Criticisms of Maslow's theory include that it is difficult to test empirically; terms such as self-actualization are difficult to measure and study.

Burton White proposed the notion of **intrinsic motivation** or the desire to perform an activity for itself because we find it inherently enjoyable. For example, a person reads several books per month because she/he finds it enjoyable. Activities carried out because of curiosity are also examples of intrinsic motivation.

Extrinsic motivation occurs when an activity is performed in order to obtain a reward or to avoid an undesirable consequence.

4.1.2 Human Needs

Motives for several of the most important human needs—hunger, thirst, sexuality—have been studied by psychologists.

What motivates us to eat? What motivates us to stop eating once we have begun? How do we know we are hungry? Psychologists have attempted to answer these and other questions related to hunger and motivation.

Researchers have found that people report that they are hungry even when their stomachs have been removed for medical reasons. The explanation for hunger, therefore, is more complex than an empty stomach. A feeling of hunger seems to be related to both the brain and body chemistry as well as to external factors.

Glucose is a simple sugar nutrient that provides energy. When the level of glucose in our bloodstream is low, we feel hungry. When glucose levels are high, we feel full. Blood glucose levels appear to be monitored by **glucostats**, neurons that are sensitive to glucose levels. Where these glucostats are located is not clear, although it seems likely that the **hypothalamus** receives messages about glucose levels.

Another body chemical, **insulin**, is also related to hunger. Insulin is important for converting blood glucose into stored fat. Insulin is a hormone secreted by the pancreas. Research has shown that insulin influences hunger indirectly by decreasing glucose levels. Research has also shown that people with elevated insulin levels report feeling hungry and usually eat more than those with normal insulin levels.

The **hypothalamus** is the brain structure that appears to be primarily responsible for food intake. Injury to the hypothalamus, for instance, can cause radical changes in eating patterns. Laboratory rats whose **lateral hypothalamus (LH,** located at the side of the hypothalamus) was damaged, would often literally starve themselves to death. When the rats' LH was stimulated, however, they would overeat.

Rats with injury to the **ventromedial hypothalamus (VMH,** located toward the center of the hypothalamus) became extreme overeaters. VMH stimulation caused animals to stop eating.

The **dual-center theory** maintains that the hypothalamus contains an "on" and an "off" switch for eating located in two different regions, the LH and VMH. These switches can be activated by internal (e.g., damage or stimulation) and external signals (e.g., sight or taste of food).

Some researchers have suggested that injury to the hypothalamus affects the weight **set point** that regulates food intake. The weight set point is the particular or target weight that the body strives to maintain. Hunger or food intake adjusts to meet this set point. This means whenever we are below our set point, we feel hungry until we gain weight to match our set point.

Set point theory has been used as one explanation for obesity. According to set point theory, each person's body has a fixed number of **fat cells,** the cells that store fat. Fat cells may shrink in size when a dieter loses weight and increase in size when weight is gained. The number of fat cells does not change, only their size changes. Some researchers propose that the shriveled fat cells that result from dieting send hunger messages to the dieter's brain.

To make matters worse, a dieter's **metabolism** (the rate at which energy is produced and expended by the body) may slow down as a result of a decrease in fat cell size. It is harder to lose weight with a slow metabolism.

Some individuals seem to naturally have a slow metabolism and even though they eat small amounts of food, they gain weight readily. Those who gain weight easily are actually biologically more efficient because they easily convert food into body tissue.

Other individuals seem to naturally have a high metabolism rate and can eat as much as they want without weight gain. These individuals are inefficient in using the food that they eat and much of it is wasted.

There is also evidence that some people have a **genetic predisposition** to become obese. It seems likely that metabolic rate is an important inherited factor.

Other reasons for eating and overeating include:

Learned preferences and habits	We learn not only when to eat and how much to eat at one time but many taste preferences are the result of experience.
External cues	External cues can influence eating. External cues can include the sight or smell of food as well as time of day.
Stress and arousal	Several research studies have shown a relationship between heightened arousal and overeating for some people.

Anorexia nervosa is an eating disorder that is characterized by an irrational pursuit of thinness and an overconcern with body image and gaining weight. Anorexics feel fat even when they look emaciated. They often are literally starving themselves to death. About 90% of people with anorexia nervosa are females.

Bulimia or **binge** eating occurs when people consume huge amounts of food in a short period of time, usually secretly. Following the binge, bulimics often engage in self-induced vomiting, vigorous exercise, laxative-abuse or other methods to **purge** themselves of the food consumed. Most bulimics maintain a normal weight.

Because we lose a significant amount of water through sweating and urination, thirst represents an important motivational drive.

Three primary internal mechanisms produce thirst. First, when the concentration of **salt cells** in the body reaches a certain level, the hypothalamus is triggered to act in a way that results in the experience of thirst.

A decrease in the total volume of fluid in the **circulatory system** also causes the sense of thirst.

Finally, a rise in body temperature or a significant energy expenditure also produces thirst, probably because of a rise in the salt concentration of the body.

The dry mouth that accompanies thirst is a symptom of the need for water but not the cause. The body does seem to have a kind of water meter in the mouth and stomach, however, that monitors the amount of water that has been consumed and immediately informs drinkers when they have had enough liquid to meet their needs.

Unlike food and water, sex is not necessary for individual survival, but is necessary for the survival of the species. Sexual motivation can arise out of social, cultural, and biological motives.

Although not essential for survival, sexual motivation is very strong in humans. Even though social and cultural factors play a more important role in human sexual behavior, **hormones** have important organizational and activational effects. In humans, the hypothalamus controls the release of **luteinizing hormone (LH)** from the **pituitary gland**. LH controls the release of masculinizing **(androgens)** and feminizing **(estrogens and progestins)** hormones from the ovaries and testes. The hypothalamus, therefore, apparently plays a role in regulating the sex drive by sensing hormone levels and affecting their secretion through pituitary gland stimulation.

Hormonal factors affect sexual behavior less in more physiologically advanced species. Hormones do control sexual behavior in lower mammals—they mate only during **ovulation** (the monthly release of an egg from the ovary) when the female secretes **pheromones**, which attract the male.

Heterosexuals are attracted to individuals of the opposite sex.

Homosexuals are attracted to individuals of the same sex.

Bisexuals are attracted to people of the same and opposite sex.

No one theory fully explains why people develop a particular sexual orientation. Some theories are **biological** in nature, suggesting that there may be a genetic or hormonal reason. Others have suggested that **environmental** factors play a key role. Still others argue that sex-role orientation is a **learned behavior**. Some feel that **childhood experiences** and **family factors** are important.

4.1.3 Achievement Motivation

Social motives are conditions that direct people toward establishing or maintaining relationships with others. Social motives are learned through socialization and cultural conditioning.

Social needs are internal conditions related to feelings about self or others and establishing and maintaining relationships.

The **need for achievement (nAch)** is a social need that directs a person to constantly strive for excellence and success.

Henry Murray identified a number of social motives or needs and believed that people have these social motives in differing degrees. He developed the **Thematic Apperception Test (TAT)** (described in chapter 3) to measure the strength of these various needs. The **need for achievement** was included on Murray's list of needs and was defined as the need to accomplish something difficult and to perform at a high standard of excellence.

David McClelland and others have been interested in the effects of high or low needs for achievement. They found that people with a **high nAch** tend to set goals of moderate difficulty. They pursue goals that are challenging yet attainable. They actively pursue present and future successes and are willing to take risks. They persist after repeated failures, plan for the future, and take pride in their success.

Achievement motivation appears to be learned and related to child-rearing practices and values in the home. Parents may be more likely to have children with high nAch if they give their children responsibilities, stress independence, and praise them for genuine accomplishments.

There is evidence that, at times, both men and women experience **fear of success**. **Fear of success** occurs when someone worries that success in competitive achievement situations will lead to unpleasant consequences (such as unpopularity).

4.2 Emotion

Emotion includes:
a subjective conscious experience or cognitive component;
bodily or physiological arousal; and
overt or behavioral expressions.

As humans, we use our emotions to **communicate** our feelings to others. Emotions are **automatic** and **involuntary**. They also guide our behavior and appear to be more complex in humans than in any other animal.

4.2.1 Elements of the Emotional Experience

Emotional reactions are associated with arousal of the **autonomic nervous system (ANS)**. The autonomic nervous system is a division of the **peripheral nervous system** that is concerned with involuntary functions of the body and regulates the activity of the glands, smooth muscles, and blood vessels. The autonomic nervous system is also responsible for the **flight-or-fight response** that occurs during emergency situations. When this response occurs, the pupils dilate, heart rate accelerates, respiration increases, adrenaline is secreted, and digestion is inhibited. The autonomic responses that accompany emotions, therefore, are controlled by the brain.

The **galvanic skin response (GSR)** describes an increase in electrical conductivity of the skin that occurs when the sweat glands increase their activity. GSR is often used as a measure of autonomic arousal and emotional reactions.

The **polygraph** or **lie detector test** is based on the assumption that there is a link between lying and emotions. Lie detector tests measure respiration, heart rate, blood pressure, and the galvanic skin response. Lie detectors do not detect lies; instead they detect **nervousness** as measured by various physiological reactions. Usually lie detectors are accurate around two-thirds of the time, but many courts do not allow lie detector evidence. This is because some people may appear nervous when they are innocent and others may appear calm even though they are guilty.

4.2.2 Theories of Emotions

Various theories have attempted to explain the experience of emotions.

William James and **Carl Lange** proposed that people experience physiological changes and interpret these changes as emotions. In other words, emotions follow behavior and not vice versa. For instance, you feel afraid after you begin to perspire. (You do not perspire because you are afraid.)

Stimulus ⟶ **Arousal/Behavior** ⟶ **Emotion**

(Snake) ⟶ (Perspiration) ⟶ (Fear)

Walter Cannon and a colleague, **P. Bard**, felt that the physiological changes in many emotional states were identical. Because of this, people cannot determine their emotional state only from their physiological state. The Cannon-Bard Theory argues that emotion occurs when the **thalamus** sends signals simultaneously to the cortex and to the autonomic nervous system.

Autonomic Arousal (Perspiration)

Stimulus ⟶ **Thalamus**

(Snake)

Emotion (Fear)

The **Common Sense Theory** argues that we **react** to emotions once they occur.

Stimulus ⟶ **Emotion** ⟶ **Reaction/Behavior**

(Snake) ⟶ (Fear) ⟶ (Perspiration)

Stanley Schachter's view of emotion is a **cognitive approach**. It is referred to as the **Schachter-Singer Theory**. This theory proposes that emotion occurs when physiological arousal causes us to search for reasons for this arousal. We examine the environment for an explanation for this arousal. Emotions are determined, therefore, by labeling our arousal based on what is occurring in our environment.

Physiological Arousal ⟶ **Appraise Environment** ⟶ **Emotion**

(Perspiration) ⟶ (A snake is present) ⟶ (Fear of snake)

or

(Perspiration) $\longrightarrow$ (I'm on a date) $\longrightarrow$ (I'm in love)

The **facial feedback theory** proposes that involuntary movements of the face send feedback to the brain about which emotion is being felt. This theory proposes that people universally show the same expressions when experiencing the same emotions. Five different universal facial expressions were suggested and include **happiness, anger, disgust, sadness**, and **fear-surprise**. For instance,

Facial expression $\longrightarrow$ **Emotion**

(Smiling) $\longrightarrow$ (Happy)

Robert Plutchik proposed that emotions evolved because they help a species to survive. He felt that emotions are:

inherited behavioral patterns, and

modified by experience.

According to Plutchik, there are eight **primary emotions: sadness, fear, surprise, anger, disgust, anticipation, joy**, and **acceptance**. Other emotions are **secondary** (or composites of primary emotions). For instance,

Surprise   +   Sadness   =   Disappointment

Fear   +   Acceptance   =   Submission

Plutchik's theory has elements of both the Common Sense Theory and Schachter's theory, as outlined below.

Stimulus event	$\longrightarrow$	**Cognitive assessment of stimulus event**	$\longrightarrow$	**Primary emotion**	$\longrightarrow$	**Behavior in response to primary emotion**
(Snake)	$\longrightarrow$	(You determine situation is dangerous.)	$\longrightarrow$	(You feel fear.)	$\longrightarrow$	(You run away.)

CHAPTER 5

Abnormal Behavior

5.1 Defining Psychological Disorders

This chapter describes how psychological disorders are defined and diagnosed and presents explanations of their possible causes.

Because it is often difficult to distinguish normal from abnormal behavior, there have been several approaches for defining **abnormal behavior**. None of the definitions presented, however, is broad enough to cover all instances of abnormal or psychological disorders.

Deviation from Average (Statistical Approach)	A statistical definition. Behaviors that are infrequent or rare are considered abnormal. The problem is that not all rare behaviors (e.g., genius) are abnormal.
Deviation from Ideal (Valuative Approach)	Considers standard behavior or what most people do. Abnormal behavior occurs when behavior deviates from the norm or what most people do. Problems with this definition are that norms change over time and people don't always agree on what ideal behavior is.
Subjective Discomfort (Personal Approach)	Behavior is abnormal if it produces distress or anxiety in an individual. A

problem with this definition is that people may be feeling no distress but may be engaging in bizarre behaviors.

Inability to Function (Practical Approach)
Inability to function effectively and adapt to the demands of society are considered symptoms of abnormal behavior according to this definition. This definition does not consider personal choice.

Insanity is a legal term and indicates that a person cannot be held responsible for his or her actions because of mental illness.

5.2 Models of Psychopathology

Psychologists use different models to understand and explain psychological disorders. A **model** is a representation that helps to organize knowledge.

Medical Model (Biological Model)
Assumes the underlying cause or **etiology** of a mental disorder has a biological basis. Views psychopathology as similar to physical illness. Medication and medical therapies are often used as treatments.

Learning Model
Abnormal behaviors are learned the same way as normal behaviors—through conditioning, reinforcements, imitation, etc. Abnormal behaviors are not considered symptoms of some underlying disease—the behaviors themselves are the problem. Treatments consist of retraining and conditioning.

Psychoanalytic Model (Psychodynamic Model)
Abnormal behaviors represent unconscious motives and conflicts. Psychoanalysis is used as treatment.

Humanistic-Existential Model (Phenomenological Model)	Abnormal behaviors occur as a result of failure to fulfill one's self-potential. Emphasizes the effects of a faulty self-image. Client-centered and Gestalt therapies are used to increase self-acceptance.
Cognitive Model	Faulty or negative thinking can cause depression or anxiety. Focus of treatment is on changing faulty, irrational, or negative thinking.

5.3 Diagnosing and Classifying Psychological Disorders

A number of schemes have been developed for classifying and diagnosing psychological disorders. No scheme is perfect, however, and all have been criticized.

One standard system that is used by most professionals is the **Diagnostic and Statistical Manual of Mental Disorders, Fourth Edition (DSM-IV),** which is published by the American Psychiatric Association. DSM-IV describes more than 300 specific mental disorders. A historical overview of the DSM:

DSM	Published in 1952 according to a format that had been used by the army during World War II.
DSM-II	In 1968 the DSM was revised to conform with different classifications used by the World Health Organization.
DSM-III	A 1977 revision that described mental disorders in greater detail.
DSM-III-R	A 1987 revision of the third edition which clarified and updated DSM-III.
DSM-IV	Published in 1994, this is the latest edition.
DSM-IV-TR	Released in 2000, this text revision saw most of its changes in Associated Features and Disorders; Specific Culture, Age, and Gender Features; Prevalence; Course; and the Familial Pattern sections.

71

DSM-IV evaluates each individual according to five dimensions or axes and is therefore considered a multiaxial system of classification.

Axis I	Describes any mental disorder or clinical syndrome that might be present.
Axis II	Describes any personality disorder that might be present.
Axis III	Describes any physical or medical disorders that might be present.
Axis IV	Rates severity of psychosocial stressors in the individual's life during the past year.
Axis V	Assesses level of adaptive functioning currently and during the past year.

The major categories of mental disorders described in DSM-IV are described in the remaining sections of this chapter.

5.4 Anxiety Disorders

Description. Intense feelings of apprehension and anxiety that impede daily functioning. Approximately 8 – 15% of adults in this country are affected by anxiety disorders.

Types. Different types of anxiety disorders include:

Generalized anxiety Disorders	Characterized by continuous, long-lasting uneasiness and tension. Person usually cannot identify a specific cause.
Panic Disorders	Recurrent attacks of overwhelming anxiety that include heart palpitations, shortness of breath, sweating, faintness, and great fear. Often referred to as **panic attacks**.
Phobic Disorders	Intense, irrational fears of specific objects or situations. Common phobias include fears of snakes, insects, spiders, and mice/

	rats. **Agoraphobia** is the fear of being in public places (or away from home) and is often associated with panic disorders.
Obsessive-Compulsive Disorders	**Obsessions** are persistent, unwanted thoughts that are unreasonable (e.g., worry over germs). **Compulsions** are repetitive behaviors performed according to certain rules or rituals (e.g., repetitive counting or checking).

Causes. No one theory or model adequately explains all cases of anxiety disorders. **Genetic factors** play a role; if one identical twin has a panic disorder, for example, there is a 30% chance that the other twin will have it also. **Chemical deficiencies** in the brain (low levels of certain **neurotransmitters**) and an overreaction to **lactic acid** may produce some kinds of anxiety disorder, especially obsessive-compulsive disorder. Anxiety can also be a **learned response** to stress. They can also be inappropriate and inaccurate **cognitions** about one's world.

5.5 Somatoform Disorders

Description. Patterns of behavior characterized by complaints of physical symptoms in the absence of any real physical illness. About 1 person in 300 has a somatoform disorder, and they are slightly more common in women than in men.

Types. Hypochondriasis and conversion disorder are the two main types of somatoform disorders.

Hypochondriasis	Involves a constant fear of illness, and normal aches and pains are misinterpreted as signs of disease.
Conversion Disorder	An appearance of a physical disturbance or illness that is caused by psychological reasons. Usually has a rapid onset. Numbness or paralysis, such as **glove anesthesia,** for example.

Cause. Conversion disorders seem to occur when an individual is under some kind of stress. The physical condition allows the person to escape or reduce the source of this stress.

5.6 Mood Disorders

Description. **Mood disorders** involve moods or emotions that are extreme and unwarranted. These disturbances in emotional feelings are strong enough to intrude on everyday living.

Types. The most serious types of mood disorders are major depression and bipolar disorders.

Major Depression	Characterized by frequent episodes of intense hopelessness, lowered self-esteem, problems concentrating and making decisions, changes in eating and sleeping patterns, fatigue, reduced sex drive, and thoughts of death. Occurs twice as frequently among females as males. Can occur at any time during the life cycle; an estimated 5 – 8% of all Americans will suffer from major depression at least once in their lifetime. Approximately one-half of people who attempt suicide are depressed.
Dysthymic Disorder	More common and less severe than major depression. Similar symptoms as major depression, but they are less intense and last for a longer period (at least two years).
Seasonal Affective Disorder (SAD)	Depressive symptoms occur during the winter months when the periods of daylight are shorter. Usually crave extra sleep and eat more carbohydrates.
Bipolar I Disorder	Characterized by two emotional extremes—depression and mania. **Mania** is

an elated, very active emotional state. Manic episodes alternate every few days, weeks, or years with periods of deep depression. Sometimes mood swings and behavior are severe enough to be classified as psychosis.

Bipolar II Disorder   Also characterized by extreme mood swings. Episodes include depression and at least one episode of **hypomania** (mania that is not severe enough to interfere with everyday life).

Cyclothymia   A slightly more common pattern of less extreme mood swings than bipolar disorder.

Causes. Both psychological and biological theories have been proposed to explain the cause of mood disorders. There is evidence that both are correct.

Traditional **psychodynamic theory** states, for example, that depression is more frequent in people with strong dependency needs and represents anger or aggression turned inward at oneself.

Other theorists have related mood disorders to cognitive or learning factors. For instance, **Martin Seligman** suggested that depression results from **learned helplessness** or a state where people feel a lack of control over their lives and believe that they cannot cope and escape from stress so they give up trying and become depressed. **Aaron Beck** proposed that faulty thinking or cognitions cause depression because depressed people typically see themselves as losers, blaming themselves when anything goes wrong. **Learning theorists** propose that depression is learned through reinforcement or imitation of depressive behaviors.

Biological factors also appear to play a role in mood disorders. For instance, there is evidence that depression can be caused by a **chemical imbalance** in the brain because the **norepinephrine** and **serotonin** systems are malfunctioning. The cyclical nature of many mood disorders suggests that abnormalities in **biological rhythms** may also play a role. **Genetics** may also play a role. This appears especially true for bipolar disorder. For example, if one member of an identical-twin pair develops bipolar disorder, 72% of the other members usually develop the disorder. Children with depressed parents are also more likely to develop depression.

5.7 Dissociative Disorders

Description. Characterized by a loss of contact with portions of consciousness or memory, resulting in disruptions in one's sense of self. They appear to be an attempt to overcome anxiety and stress by dissociating oneself from the core of one's personality and result in a loss of memory, identity, or consciousness.

Types. The major dissociative disorders are:

Psychogenic Amnesia	Either partial or total memory loss that can last from a few hours to many years. Usually remembers nonthreatening aspects of life. There appears to be no physical cause but often results from stress. (That is, one "doesn't remember" stressful aspects of one's life.)
Psychogenic Fugue	People suddenly leave or "flee" their present life and establish a new, different existence and identity in a new location. Their former life is blocked from memory. Often they return from their fugue state to their former life just as suddenly as they left.
Multiple Personality Disorder	One person develops two or more distinct personalities.

Cause. Dissociative disorders allow people to escape from an anxiety producing situation. The person either produces a new personality to deal with the stress, or the situation that caused the stress is forgotten or left behind. For instance, researchers have found that about 94% of people with multiple personalities were abused as children. Not all abused children, however, exhibit multiple personalities.

76

5.8 Personality Disorders

Description. **Personality disorders** are patterns of traits that are long-standing, maladaptive, and inflexible and keep a person from functioning properly in society. Behavior often disrupts social relationships. Personality disorders are coded on **Axis II** of the **DSM-IV** system for diagnosing mental disorders (see section 5.3 above).

Types. Representative types of personality disorders are described below.

Antisocial Displays no regard for moral or ethical rules and continuously violates the rights of others. Is manipulative, impulsive, and lacks feelings for others. Also appears to lack a conscience or guilt.

Narcissistic An exaggerated sense of self and self-importance; preoccupied with fantasies of success. Lacks empathy. Often expects special treatment.

Paranoid Continual unjustified suspicion and mistrust of people. Often appears cold and unemotional. Easily offended.

Histrionic Overreacts and overdramatic in response to minor situations. Often seen as vain, shallow, dependent, or manipulative.

Avoidant Tends to be a "loner," or social snob. Oversensitive to rejection or possible humiliation. Has low self-esteem.

Schizotypal Not disturbed enough to be diagnosed as schizophrenic. Strangeness in thinking, speech, and behavior.

Causes. Suggested causes for personality disorders range from problems in family relationships to a biological inability to experience emotions. A growing body of evidence indicates that biological problems may be the cause of many personality disorders.

5.9 Schizophrenic Disorders

Description. **Schizophrenia** is a serious **psychotic disorder** (i.e., one is out-of-touch with reality). Schizophrenia is **NOT** the same as multiple personality disorder described previously with the dissociative disorders. Schizophrenia includes **disorders of thought.** Schizophrenics display problems in both how they think and what they think.

Schizophrenic thinking is often **incoherent.** For instance, they sometimes use **neologisms** or words that only have meaning to the person speaking them (e.g., the word "glump"). **Loose associations,** where thought appears logically unconnected, is another characteristic that is sometimes seen. **Word salad** describes a jumble of words that are spoken that do not make sense.

The **content** of a schizophrenic's thinking is also disturbed. Various kinds of delusions are common. **Delusions** are false beliefs that are maintained even though they are clearly out of touch with reality. Common delusions are beliefs that they are being controlled by someone else, that someone is out to get them, that they are a famous person from history (e.g., the President of the United States), and that their thoughts are being broadcast so that others are able to know what they are thinking.

A person with schizophrenia may also experience **hallucinations** or the experience of perceiving things that do not actually exist. The most common hallucination is hearing voices that do not exist.

Schizophrenics also tend to display **flat** (absent) or **inappropriate affect.** Even dramatic events tend to produce little or no emotional reaction from a schizophrenic. The emotional responses they do display often are bizarre and unexpected.

A person with schizophrenia usually has little interest in others and appears **socially withdrawn.**

Abnormal motor behavior may also occur, such as unusual pacing back and forth, rocking constantly, or being immobilized for long periods of time.

Schizophrenia usually involves a noticeable **deterioration in functioning.** That is, the person used to function adaptively (and did not display symptoms of schizophrenia) but now the quality of work, social relations, and personal care have deteriorated. Their previous level of functioning has broken down.

Types. Five major subtypes of schizophrenia are described in DSM-IV.

Disorganized	Severe deterioration of adaptive behavior. Speech incoherent. Strange facial grimaces common. Inappropriate silliness, babbling, giggling, and obscene behavior may be displayed. Includes 5% of schizophrenics.
Catatonic	Characterized by disordered movement. Alternates between extreme withdrawal where the body is kept very still and extreme excitement where movement is rapid and speech incoherent. **Waxy flexibility** describes the odd posturing. Makes up about 8% of all cases.
Paranoid	Delusions of persecution or grandeur. Judgment is impaired and unpredictable. Often includes anxiety, anger, jealousy, or argumentativeness. Hallucinations are common. Tends to appear later in life than the other types. Onset is often sudden. Less impaired. Makes up about 40% of all schizophrenics.
Undifferentiated	No one subtype dominates. About 40% of all schizophrenics receive this diagnosis.
Residual	Has had a prior episode of schizophrenia but currently is not displaying major symptoms. Subtle indications of schizophrenia may be observed, however.

Causes. Genetic, biological, psychological, and environmental factors have been used to explain the origin of schizophrenia. No one theory, however, can adequately account for all forms of schizophrenia.

Twin studies have suggested a **hereditary** or **genetic** component to schizophrenia. When one identical twin is identified as schizophrenic, the other twin has a 42 – 48% chance of also developing schizophrenia. Children of schizophrenics who are adopted by nonschizophrenics also have a higher incidence of schizophrenia than control populations. Schizophrenia, therefore, does run in families.

Most people with schizophrenic relatives, however, do not develop schizophrenia. This has led researchers to conclude that what might be inherited is a **predisposition** or genetic **vulnerability** for schizophrenia. What is needed for schizophrenia to develop is this genetic predisposition plus environmental stress. This is often referred to as the **predisposition** or **vulnerability model** and the **diathesis-stress model**.

Neurochemical factors are also related to schizophrenia. Schizophrenia appears to be accompanied by changes in the activity of one or more **neurotransmitters** in the brain. The **dopamine hypothesis** suggests that schizophrenia occurs when there is excess activity in those areas of the brain using dopamine to transmit nerve impulses. Excessive dopamine appears related to delusions.

Some researchers have suggested that **structural abnormalities in the brain** are linked to schizophrenia. Studies have suggested that schizophrenic individuals have difficulty focusing their attention and display bizarre behaviors because of brain abnormalities. Such structural abnormalities might include shrinking or deterioration of cells in the cerebral cortex that cause enlargements of the brain's fluid-filled ventricles, reduced blood flow in parts of the brain, and abnormalities in **brain lateralization** or in the ways the hemispheres of the brain communicate with each other.

Psychoanalytic theorists propose that schizophrenia represents a regression to earlier stages in life when the id was the most dominant aspect of personality.

Other theorists assert that schizophrenia is a learned behavior and consists of a set of inappropriate responses to social stimuli. This is sometimes referred to as the **learned-inattention theory**. Defective or faulty communication patterns within the family may also be learned and therefore result in schizophrenia. Such faulty communication might include unintelligible speech, stories with no ending, extensive contradictions, and poor attention to child's attempts at communicating.

The **two-strike theory** suggests a prenatal link to schizophrenia. According to this theory, the **first strike** is an inherited susceptibility of the fetal brain to be disrupted by exposure to the flu virus during the second trimester of pregnancy. The **second strike** occurs when exposure to the flu virus actually occurs during the second trimester of pregnancy. Microscopic examination of the brains of schizophrenics does indicate that whatever is going wrong in their brains probably occurred during the second trimester of pregnancy.

It appears, therefore, that schizophrenia is associated with several possible causes. Schizophrenia is probably not caused by a single factor but by a combination of interrelated variables.

CHAPTER 6

Psychotherapy

6.1 Therapy

Psychotherapy is the treatment of emotional and behavioral problems through psychological techniques. Psychotherapy uses psychological rather than biological approaches to treatment. Psychotherapy involves conversation or verbal interactions between a person with a psychological disorder and someone who has been trained to help correct that disorder, a **therapist**.

Historically, one early approach to treating mental illness used by Stone Age society was **trepanning** or boring a hole in the skull of the patient. Needless to say, many did not survive this primitive procedure.

During the Middle Ages, treatment focused on **demonology** or blaming supernatural forces for the mentally ill. **Exorcism** was used to drive out the evil.

Following the French Revolution in 1792, **Philippe Pinel** reformed the ways that patients were treated in mental hospitals by arguing for more humane treatments.

By the mid-1800s, many began to realize that abnormal behavior could result from damage to the brain and central nervous system. Over the years there has been an explosive growth in the number of therapies available to treat mental illness. General descriptions of the various types of therapies and therapeutic techniques that have been developed include:

Insight Therapy	Any psychotherapy where the goal is to help clients better understand themselves, their situation, or their problems.
Action Therapy	This therapy focuses on directly changing a troubling habit or behavior.
Directive Therapy	Any approach in which the therapist provides strong guidance during therapy sessions.
Nondirective Therapy	A therapeutic technique in which clients assume responsibility for solving their own problems. The therapist creates a supportive atmosphere so this can happen.
Individual Therapy	A therapy session involving one client and one therapist.
Group Therapy	A therapy session that includes several clients at one time and one or more therapists. One particular problem or difficulty is usually the focus (e.g., alcoholism or eating disorders).
Family Therapy	An approach that focuses on the family as a whole unit. The goal is to avoid labeling a single family member as the focus of therapy; each person's contribution to the group is the focus.
Outpatient Therapy	Clients receive psychotherapy while they live in the community.
Inpatient Therapy	Clients receive psychotherapy while in a hospital or other residential institution.

Therapists represent a variety of theoretical orientations and professional backgrounds. The major professionals involved in psychotherapy are described in the table that follows.

Type	Degree	Description
Clinical or Counseling Psychologists	Ph.D. or Psy.D.	Trained to diagnose, test, and treat individuals with psychological disorders.
Psychiatrists	M.D.	Medical doctors who specialize in treating psychological disorders. They can prescribe medication.
Social Workers	M.S.W.	Have a Masters of Social Work degree and specialize in counseling and therapy.
Psychoanalysts	M.D. or Ph.D.	Usually psychiatrists, but can be psychologists who are trained in the psychoanalytic techniques of Sigmund Freud.
Psychiatric Nurses	B.S.N. or M.A./M.S.	Usually work with patients while they are hospitalized for psychiatric care.
Counselors	M.A. or M.S.	Usually provide supportive therapy, family therapy, or drug and alcohol abuse counseling.

6.2 Insight Therapies

As stated above, the goal of **insight therapies** is for clients to gain insight or increased understanding of themselves in order to promote changes in personality and behavior. There are at least 200 different insight therapies available today. The more popular ones are described in the following sections.

6.2.1 Traditional Psychoanalysis

Psychoanalysis is an insight therapy that emphasizes the understanding of unconscious conflicts, motives, and defense mechanisms.

Traditional psychoanalysis was developed by **Sigmund Freud** (see chapter 2 for an overview of Freud's theory of personality).

At first Freud and his colleague **Joseph Breuer** tried to use **hypnosis** either to help patients or clients recall events from their pasts or to cure them by using **hypnotic suggestion.**

When hypnosis proved unsuccessful, Freud had patients relax on a couch and merely talk about their memories. This came to be known as the **talking cure.**

Freud treated people who seemed to have phobias, panic disorders, obsessive-compulsive disorders, and conversion disorders. He referred to these disorders as **neuroses**. Freud felt that neurotic disorders were caused by unconscious conflicts that were left over from early childhood. He concluded that the neurotic or **hysterical** symptoms displayed by his patients developed out of these unconscious conflicts, wishes, and fantasies from their childhoods.

The goal of traditional psychoanalysis is to help patients gain insight into their unconscious thoughts and emotions and to understand how these unconscious elements affect their everyday life. Treatment may require many sessions per week over the course of several years.

Psychoanalysts seek to maintain a **neutral relationship** with clients so the clients can reveal their unresolved unconscious conflicts. Techniques used by traditional psychoanalysts include:

Free Association	Patients do not censor their thoughts or words but are encouraged to spontaneously say whatever comes to their mind. In order to encourage this, patients relax by lying on a couch, facing away from the analyst.
Dream Analysis	Freud felt that dreams were "the royal road to the unconscious," whereby the id feels free to reveal itself. The **manifest content** of dreams is what the patient actually remembers about the dream. The **latent content** is what the dream symbolizes. Psychoanalysts help interpret the

	latent content for patients.
Interpretations	Psychoanalysts offer insights or alternative ways of looking at dreams, thoughts, and behaviors based on possible unconscious needs and desires.
Defense Mechanisms	Throughout therapy, analysts look for signs of possible defense mechanisms (described in chapter 2).
Transference	Analysts believe if they maintain a neutral relationship with patients and reveal nothing about themselves, transference will develop. Transference occurs when patients transfer to the therapist's perceptions and feelings about other people (e.g., their parents). Possible signs of transference include falling in love or being hostile with the therapist.
Resistance	Resistance involves any unconscious behaviors by the patient that hinder the progress of therapy. Some examples include being late for therapy sessions, missing sessions, or becoming angry at the therapist.

Critics of psychoanalysis argue that treatment is expensive and requires good verbal skills on the part of the client. It is also basically untestable and difficult to measure scientifically.

6.2.2 Modern Psychoanalysis

The term **psychodynamic** is often used to refer to a variety of approaches that descended from Freud's theory and were developed by **neo-Freudians** (see chapter 2). Examples include **ego analysis, interpersonal therapy, individual analysis,** and **object relations therapy.**

Psychodynamic therapies differ from traditional psychoanalysis in several important ways:

- Many do not use the Freudian "couch" but rather sit face-to-face with their patients.

- They explore conscious thoughts and feelings as much as unconscious ones and, therefore, focus on current problems as well as childhood conflicts.

- They emphasize the concept of working through or developing new behaviors and emotions following insight.

- Their therapy is often more streamlined—does not require as many sessions per week nor as many total sessions and is, therefore, often less expensive.

- Some therapists have developed techniques to use with children.

6.2.3 Humanistic Therapies

Humanistic therapies (sometimes called **phenomenological**) are also insight-oriented therapies. The humanist view is optimistic and the emphasis of therapy is on fulfilling one's potential. Client-Centered, Gestalt, and Existential are forms of humanistic therapy.

Carl Rogers founded **client-centered** or **person-centered therapy**. This therapy attempts to focus on the person's own point of view, instead of the therapist's interpretations. Therefore, the client, or person, is the center of the process and determines what will be discussed during each session. The therapist's role is nondirective during the therapy process.

Techniques used in client-centered therapy include:

Unconditional positive regard	The client is accepted totally by the therapist. The therapist always portrays a positive, nonjudgmental attitude toward the client.
Empathy	The therapist attempts to see the world through the client's eyes in order to

	achieve an accurate understanding of the client's emotions.
Congruence	Also known as **genuineness** or **realness**. Therapist does not maintain a formal attitude, but rather expresses what she/he genuinely feels—strives to be **authentic**.
Reflection	Technique whereby the therapist serves as a psychological "mirror" by communicating back to the client a summary of what was said or what emotion the client seems to be expressing.
Active listening	Technique in which therapist attempts to understand both the content and emotion of a client's statements.

The goal of **Gestalt therapy** is for clients to become aware of what they are doing and how they can change, while learning to accept and value themselves. This therapy is most often associated with **Fritz Perls**. The word Gestalt means **whole** or complete. The Gestalt therapist helps individuals rebuild thinking and feeling into connected wholes. Gestalt therapy is more **directive** than either client-centered therapy or existential therapy.

Working either one-to-one in individual therapy or in a group therapy setting, the Gestalt therapist encourages individuals to become more aware of their immediate experience. The emphasis is on what is happening here and now rather than what happened in the past or what may happen in the future. It focuses on what really exists rather than on what is absent and on what is real rather than on what is fantasy. The therapist also helps promote awareness by drawing attention to the client's voice, posture, and movements. Gestalt therapists often confront and challenge clients with evidence of their defensiveness, game playing, etc.

Existential therapy is a humanistic approach to therapy that addresses the meaning of life and allows clients to devise a system of values that gives purpose to their lives. It is based on the premise that the inability to deal with freedom can produce anguish, fear, and concern. The goal of therapy is for clients to come to grips with the freedoms they have, to understand how they fit in with the rest of the world, and to give them more meaning for their lives. The importance of free choice or free will is emphasized.

The existential therapist may be directive in therapy to probe and challenge clients' views of the world. **Confrontation** may be used whereby clients are challenged to examine the quality of their existence. When successful, existential therapy often brings about a reappraisal of what is important in life.

6.2.4 Cognitive Therapies

Cognitive therapies are insight therapies that emphasize recognizing and changing negative thoughts and maladaptive beliefs. Cognitive therapists argue that people have psychological disorders because their thinking is inappropriate or maladaptive. The goal of therapy is to change or restructure clients' thinking.

Cognitive-behavior therapy is a blending of behavioral therapy (described in section 6.3) and cognitive therapy.

Albert Ellis and Aaron Beck are the two best known cognitive therapists.

Rational-Emotive Therapy (RET) was developed by **Albert Ellis**. RET encourages people to examine their beliefs carefully and rationally, to make positive statements about themselves, and to solve problems effectively.

Rational-emotive therapy is based on Ellis' **ABC theory**. A refers to the **activating** event, **B** to the person's **belief** about the event, and **C** to the emotional **consequence** that follows. Ellis claimed that **A** does not cause **C**, but instead **B** causes **C**. If the **belief** is irrational, then the emotional consequence can be extreme distress.

Ellis felt that many beliefs are irrational. For instance, many people hold irrational **should beliefs** (e.g., "I **should** be perfect!"). Because it is impossible to live up to these irrational "should" beliefs, people are doomed to frustration and unhappiness.

Rational-emotive therapy is a **directive, confrontational** form of therapy that is designed to challenge clients' irrational beliefs about themselves and others. It helps clients replace irrational beliefs with rational ones that are appropriate and less distressing. Rational-emotive therapists do not believe that a warm relationship between therapist and client is necessary for the therapy to be effective.

Another cognitive therapy that focuses on irrational beliefs is that of **Aaron Beck**. Beck's theory assumes that depression and anxiety are caused by people's distorted views of reality. These distorted views cause clients to have negative views of the world, others, and themselves. Beck felt that many depressed and anxious people have **automatic thoughts** or unreasonable ideas that rule their lives.

The goal of therapy, according to Beck, is to help clients stop their negative thoughts and to help them develop realistic thinking about the situations they encounter. The therapist challenges clients' irrational thoughts, and clients are often given homework assignments, such as keeping track of automatic thoughts and then substituting more rational thoughts.

6.2.5 Evaluating Insight Therapies

It is difficult to evaluate the effectiveness of any psychotherapy. For instance, **spontaneous remission** sometimes occurs when psychological disorders clear up on their own without treatment or therapy. Because of the possibility of spontaneous remission, if clients seem to "get better" after therapy, you cannot automatically assume that this recovery was due to the treatment.

Judging the effectiveness of insight therapies is especially difficult because it is often unclear what to measure and who to ask. For instance, do you ask the client or the therapist? Do you measure behavior or emotions?

Results from **meta-analysis**, a mathematical technique that summarizes the outcomes of many different studies, indicate that insight therapy results in a better outcome than no treatment about 75 to 80% of the time. Only a few clients (around 10%) are worse off after therapy.

Individuals who seem to have the best response to insight therapies are intelligent, successful people. These are individuals who are also highly motivated and who have positive attitudes about therapy. Clients who are less severely disturbed are more likely to benefit than those with more severe pathology.

6.3 Behavioral Therapies

Behavioral therapies are based on the assumption that both normal and abnormal behaviors are learned. Treatment consists, therefore, of either learning a new "normal" behavior or unlearning a maladaptive behavior. Behavior therapies are built upon classical and operant conditioning as well as imitation and social learning. Behavioral therapies are often referred to as **behavior modification**.

6.3.1 Types of Therapies

Several therapies based on classical conditioning, operant or instrumental conditioning, and social learning have been developed.

Classical conditioning occurs whenever a neutral stimulus acquires the ability to evoke a response that was originally triggered by another stimulus. Systematic desensitization and aversion therapy are two therapies based on the classical conditioning approach.

Systematic desensitization is a behavior therapy used to reduce clients' anxiety and fear responses through counterconditioning. **Counterconditioning** is a process of reconditioning in which a person is taught a new, more adaptive response to a stimulus. For instance, instead of displaying a fear response when confronted with a frightening situation, clients are counterconditioned to display a relaxed response.

Systematic desensitization is a three-step process:

Step 1 The therapist and client construct a **hierarchy of fears**. The client ranks (from the least amount to the greatest amount of fear) specific situations that arouse anxiety.

Step 2 The client is trained in relaxation techniques.

Step 3 The client works through the hierarchy of fears while practicing the relaxation techniques learned in Step 2.

Systematic desensitization is based on the premise that anxiety and relaxation are incompatible responses. It has proven very effective in dealing with fears, phobias, and anxiety.

Flooding is another behavioral technique used to help clients overcome fears, and it is almost the opposite of systematic desensitization. During flooding, clients are exposed to the fear all at once for an extended period until their anxiety decreases. Flooding can be successful because it shows clients that none of the dreaded consequences they expect actually happen.

Aversion therapy is another therapy based on classical conditioning. It is also a form of counterconditioning that pairs an aversive or noxious stimulus with a stimulus that elicits an undesired behavior. For instance, aversion therapy has been used to treat alcoholics. The therapist might administer a drug that causes nausea and vomiting whenever alcohol is consumed. By pairing the drug with alcohol, the therapist hopes to create a conditioned aversion to alcohol.

Operant or **instrumental conditioning** occurs whenever voluntary responses come to be controlled by their consequences. Token economies, contingency contracting, time-out, extinction, and punishment are therapeutic approaches based on operant conditioning.

Token economies	Desired behaviors are rewarded with tokens that can later be exchanged for desired objects or privileges. Clients are "fined" (i.e., must return some tokens) for inappropriate behaviors. Often used in institutional settings, such as schools, hospitals, etc.
Contingency contracting	A written agreement is drawn up between the therapist and client that states behavioral objectives the client hopes to attain. Contracts usually state positive consequences or rewards for meeting the objectives and sometimes include negative consequences if goals are not met.
Time-out	Used to eliminate undesirable behavior, usually with children. It involves moving the individual away from all reinforcement for a period of time.

Extinction	Occurs when a maladaptive behavior is not followed by reinforcers. Often involves ignoring a behavior.
Punishment	Occurs when behavior is followed by an aversive stimulus. The goal is to eliminate the inappropriate behavior and is often combined with positive reinforcement for appropriate behavior.

Observational Learning and Modeling occurs when children and adults learn behaviors by observing others. According to **Albert Bandura**, modeling is most effective for learning new behavior by helping to eliminate fears (by watching others engage in the feared behavior or interact with the feared object) and encouraging the expression of already existing behavior.

People can also learn inappropriate or maladaptive behaviors by observing others.

Participant modeling is a technique that occurs when the model not only demonstrates the appropriate behavior in graduated steps, but the client attempts to imitate the model step by step. The therapist provides encouragement and support.

Social skills training is a behavioral therapy designed to improve interpersonal skills and emphasizes modeling, behavioral rehearsal, and shaping.

6.3.2 Evaluating Behavioral Therapies

Behavioral therapies appear to be the most successful with certain kinds of problems. For instance, they have been reported to work well for phobias, compulsive behaviors, controlling impulses, and learning new social skills to replace maladaptive ones.

Behavioral therapies have been criticized because they emphasize external behavior and ignore internal thoughts and expectations. Behavioral therapies have also been criticized for focusing on the symptom, without searching for what it might symbolize. Additionally, they are not well suited to treat some types of problems.

6.4   Biological Treatments

The **biological perspective** views abnormal behavior as a symptom of an underlying physical disorder and usually favors biological therapy.

6.4.1   Drug Treatments

Psychopharmacotherapy is the treatment of mental disorders with medication. This is often referred to as **drug therapy**. Drugs used to treat mental disorders are categorized based on their effects and are described below.

Antipsychotics (Neuropleptics)	Gradually reduce psychotic symptoms, such as hallucinations, delusions, paranoia, disordered thinking, and incoherence. Between 60 – 70% show improvement when taking these drugs. *Side-effects* include drowsiness, constipation, dry mouth, muscular rigidity, and impaired coordination. Can cause **tardive dyskinesia** or permanent chronic tremors and involuntary muscle movements. *Examples*: Haldol, Mellaril, Thorazine, and Clozapine.
Antidepressants (Thymoleptics)	Designed to relieve symptoms of depression. About 60 – 70% of patients who take these drugs report an improved mood. Depressive symptoms are not affected until about two weeks after drug therapy begins. *Side-effects* can include sleepiness and may be dangerous if mixed with alcohol. *Examples*: Tofranil, Elavil, Prozac, Anafranil, and Nardil.
Antianxiety Drugs (Anxiolytics)	Commonly called **tranquilizers**, these mood – altering substances are calming, reduce anxiety and stress, and lower excitability. They are the most widely prescribed of

all legal drugs.

Side-effects: Some can cause physical dependence and withdrawal symptoms if abruptly discontinued.

Examples: Librium, Valium, Xanax, BuSpar, Equanil, Miltown, and Tranxene.

Antimania Drug (Lithium)

If taken regularly, **lithium carbonate** is about 80% effective in preventing both the depression and mania associated with bipolar disorder. Dosage must be exact and constantly monitored, however, because too little has no effect and too much can be deadly. It takes a week or two of regular use before results are evident.

Side-effects: Vomiting, nausea, tremor, fatigue, slurred speech; overdose can result in death.

Examples: Lithium carbonate and Eskalith.

6.4.2 Electroconvulsive Therapy (ECT)

In 1938 Italian physicians **Ugo Cerletti** and **Lucio Bini** created seizures in patients by passing an electric current through their brains. During the 1940s and 1950s **electroconvulsive therapy (ECT)** or **shock treatment** was routinely used to treat depression, schizophrenia, and sometimes mania. It was often used on patients who did not need it. Today ECT is an uncommon treatment and is used mainly as a last resort treatment for severe depression. No one knows for sure how or why ECT works. The seizure that results from ECT may temporarily change the biochemical balance in the brain, which results in a decrease of depressive symptoms. The effects of ECT are only temporary if not followed by drug therapy and psychotherapy. Up to 100,000 people receive ECT each year.

Typically, patients are anesthetized and given a muscle relaxant. ECT occurs by placing two electrodes on a patient's head and sending a mild electric current through the brain for one or two seconds. Immediately after the shock, the patient loses consciousness and

95

experiences a seizure that lasts up to one minute. The entire ECT procedure takes about five minutes and the risk of death or any medical complication is very rare. However, there is a potential for memory loss and a decreased ability to learn and retain new information for up to several weeks following the procedure.

6.4.3 Psychosurgery

Psychosurgery is brain surgery and is even a more drastic procedure than ECT described above. Psychosurgery is performed to relieve the symptoms of serious psychological disorders, such as severe depression, severe obsessions or anxiety, and, in some cases, of unbearable chronic pain. It is not the same as brain surgery that is performed to correct a physical problem.

In 1937, **Egas Moniz** introduced a surgical technique called **prefrontal lobotomy**. In the 1940s and 1950s prefrontal lobotomies were routinely performed during which the frontal lobes of the brain were surgically separated from the deeper brain centers involved in emotion. No brain tissue was removed. Eventually it became apparent that this surgery often left patients in a severely deteriorated condition (i.e., impaired intellect, loss of motivation, personality changes) and was no cure-all for mental illness.

The advent of antipsychotic drugs in the mid-1950s ended most psychosurgery. Today, psychosurgery is performed only in rare cases where all else has failed and involves the destruction of only a tiny amount of brain tissue.

6.5 Community Mental Health

Community psychology is a movement that attempts to minimize or prevent mental disorders, not just treat them. Rather than emphasizing hospitalization or one-on-one therapy sessions, the community psychology approach focuses on the **prevention** of psychological disorders.

During the 1960s, the mental health system adopted a program of **deinstitutionalization**, discharging people from mental hospitals into the community, hopefully into a supportive environment of family and friends. The efforts to integrate the chronically mentally ill into the community have, for the most part, failed.

The community mental health approach argues that effective treatment for mental illness requires a variety of different organizations and services. These include **crisis hotlines, family consultation** and **family therapy, halfway houses, long-term outpatient care**, some **short-term inpatient care, job training, day care**, and other supportive services.

CHAPTER 7

Social Behavior

7.1 Attitudes and Attitude Change

Social psychology is the branch of psychology concerned with the way individuals' thoughts, feelings, and behaviors are influenced by others.

Social cognition involves the mental processes associated with how people perceive and react to others.

Attitudes are beliefs and opinions that can predispose individuals to behave in certain ways.

Social psychologists have defined **three components** of attitudes:

Cognitive Component   Includes the beliefs and ideas held about the object of an attitude.

Affective Component   The emotional feelings stimulated by an attitude.

Behavioral Component   The predispositions to act in certain ways that are relevant to one's attitude.

The relationship between attitudes and behavior is complicated. You cannot predict specific behavior by knowing someone's attitude. **Situational demands** and **constraints** may lead to inconsistent relationships between attitudes and behavior.

The **mere exposure effect** predicts that our attitude toward something or someone will become more positive with continued exposure.

7.1.1 Cognitive Dissonance

Cognitive dissonance is the conflict that arises when a person holds two or more attitudes that are inconsistent. Cognitive dissonance theory was developed by social psychologist **Leon Festinger**. When in a state of cognitive dissonance, Festinger suggested we feel uneasy and are thereby motivated to make our attitudes consistent.

An example of dissonant cognitions would be, "I smoke, yet I believe that smoking is unhealthy." Festinger's theory predicts that these two thoughts would lead to a state of cognitive dissonance. Efforts to reduce this dissonance will probably cause attitudes to change. This could reduce dissonance by one of the following:

Modifying one or both of the cognitions.
Example: "I really don't smoke that much."

Changing the perceived importance of one of the cognitions.
Example: "Most of the research is done with laboratory rats and rats seem to get cancer from everything."

Adding cognitions.
Example: "I exercise more than the average person and eat healthy foods."

Denying the two cognitions are related to each other.
Example: "I don't know anyone who has died from lung cancer."

Festinger and **Carlsmith** in 1959 demonstrated cognitive dissonance in a classic experiment. In one condition, subjects were offered $1 to describe a dull, boring task as interesting. A control group was offered $20 to describe the task as interesting. Festinger and Carlsmith reasoned that subjects paid $20 to tell a lie would not experience dissonance because they had a good reason or justification for their behavior—$20. Subjects paid $1, however, should experience cognitive dissonance because they told a lie for little justification. Just as they predicted, subjects paid $1 actually rated the task as more enjoyable, thereby reducing their dissonance, than subjects who were paid $20.

Effort justification is another example of cognitive dissonance.

We tend to rate more favorably those experiences, items, etc., that require more effort to obtain. **Aronson** and **Mills** in 1959 demonstrated effort justification by finding that college students who went through a more severe initiation in order to join what turned out to be a boring group, later rated the group as more enjoyable than did a group that did not go through any initiation.

Selective exposure occurs when we attempt to minimize dissonance by exposing ourselves only to information that supports a choice we have made.

An alternative theoretical explanation for cognitive dissonance was suggested by **Darryl Bem**. Bem's **self-perception** theory states that people form attitudes by observing their own behavior and by applying the same principles to themselves as they do to others. That is, when we are unclear about the reasons we have engaged in a certain behavior, we look at our behavior and try to figure out why we did what we did. For instance, if I agreed to say a boring task was interesting for only a dollar, the task must have been interesting or else I wouldn't have done it.

7.1.2 Persuasion

Persuasion occurs when others attempt to change our attitudes. The process of persuasion includes four basic elements: source, receiver, message, and channel.

1. **The source (or communicator)**
   The source or communicator is the individual who delivers a persuasive message. Communicators are most influential when they have **expertise, credibility, trustworthiness**, and **power. Attractiveness** and **similarity** to the target audience are also important.

2. **The receiver (target or audience)**
   The receiver, target, or audience is the person to whom a persuasive message is sent. Although the magnitude of differences between women and men is not large, some research suggests that women are more easily persuaded than men.

Younger individuals are more likely to change their attitudes than older individuals. If the receiver is not strongly committed to a preexisting attitude, change is more likely. A **latitude of acceptance** is a range of potentially acceptable positions on an issue, centered on one's initial attitude position. A message that falls within a receiver's latitude of acceptance is much more likely to be persuasive. Information from a persuasive message is processed via a **central route** when the receiver carefully ponders the content and logic of the message. **Peripheral route processing** is taken when persuasion depends on nonmessage factors, such as the attractiveness and credibility of the source and emotional responses. Research suggests that central route processing results in the most lasting attitude change.

3. **Message factors**

   The message is the information transmitted by the source. The less informed we are or the more frightened we are, the more we will be influenced by an emotional message. Positive emotional appeals can be successful, especially through music. **Two-sided arguments** in which both sides of an issue are presented seem to be more effective than one-sided presentations. One-sided messages work when the audience is uneducated about the issue.

4. **The channel or medium**

   The channel is the medium through which the message is sent. Television may be the most powerful medium.

7.2 Person Perception

Person perception relates to how we form **impressions** of others.

A **person scheme** or **social scheme** is an organized cluster of information, ideas, or impressions about a person. These schemes are not always accurate, however, and can be influenced by physical appearance, first impressions, and stereotypes.

7.2.1 Physical Appearance

In general, studies have shown that people have a bias toward viewing attractive men and women as intelligent, competent, talented, pleasant, interesting, kind, and sensitive.

However, people sometimes downplay the talent of successful women who happen to be attractive, attributing their success to their good looks instead of their competence.

7.2.2 First Impressions

First impressions can be powerful and can influence many of the later impressions we form about people.

The **primacy effect** is the tendency for early information (i.e., first impressions) to be considered more important than later information about a person when forming impressions. By relying on our first impressions, we do not pay close attention to later information and our first impression becomes a framework through which later impressions are formed.

The primacy effect is helpful in simplifying our impressions if the people we are judging really are consistent.

The primacy effect can lead to person perception errors, however, if the people we are judging are inconsistent in their behavior.

The primacy effect can lead to a **self-fulfilling prophecy** where our expectations influence people to act in ways that confirm our original expectations.

7.2.3 Stereotypes, Prejudice, and Discrimination

Stereotypes are broad overgeneralizations and widely held beliefs about the way a group of people think and act. The most common stereotypes in our society are based on sex and membership in ethnic and occupational groups. Stereotypes can be positive and negative.

Prejudice is a negative attitude toward a group of people that is made without sufficient evidence and is not easily changed. Prejudice includes preconceived hostile and irrational feelings.

Discrimination involves action against a person or group of people based on race, ethnicity, class, sex, etc. Discrimination is usually based on prejudice.

Over 40 years ago, **Adorno** and his colleagues wrote that people who are highly prejudiced tend to have **authoritarian personalities**—they tend to be submissive and obedient to authority and to reject other groups in a punitive way. Authoritarian personalities tend to divide people into **in-groups** or **out-groups** and often had harsh and punitive parents. Adorno developed the **California F scale** to measure authoritarianism.

The **scapegoat theory** of stereotypes proposed that people who are frustrated and unhappy about something will choose a relatively powerless group to take the blame for a situation that is not their fault.

The **social identity theory** proposed that we favor the groups to which we belong in order to enhance our self-esteem.

The **cognitive approach to stereotypes** proposed that the tendency to divide people into social groups is a normal cognitive process. They help us simplify and organize our world. Stereotypes can guide the way we perceive people, make attributions for their behavior, remember them, and evaluate them.

Prejudice can be overcome through education, legislation, and bringing groups into contact with one another to work toward a common goal.

7.3 Attribution Process

Attributions are inferences that people draw about the causes of events, others' behavior, and their own behavior. We make attributions because we want to understand our own behavior, the behavior of others, and the events that take place in our lives. We are most likely to make attributions when:

unusual events grab our attention;

events have personal consequences for us; and

others behave in unexpected ways.

We can classify attributions in a number of ways. One basic distinction is between **internal causes** (a person's personality traits or motives) or **external causes** (environmental or situational factors).

7.3.1 Factors Influencing Attributions

Harold Kelley proposed three factors that influence whether we make internal (person) attributions or external (situational) attributions:

Consensus	The degree to which someone's behavior is similar to other's behavior.
Distinctiveness	Whether the person is responding in a unique way in this situation but would respond differently in other situations.
Consistency	Whether the person responds in the same way on most occasions.

Low consensus + low distinctiveness + high consistency = **Internal** (person) **attribution**.

High consensus + high distinctiveness + high consistency = **External** (situational) **attribution**.

7.3.2 Fundamental Attribution Error

The **fundamental attribution error** refers to the tendency to attribute other's behavior to internal (personal) causes (e.g., I attribute my roommate's poor test performance to a lack of ability).

We also tend to overestimate external (situational) causes when explaining our own behavior (e.g., I attribute my poor test performance to a lack of effort). This is sometimes referred to as the **actor-observer bias**. According to the actor-observer bias, we make the fundamental attribution error in judging others, but not when judging ourselves.

We may consider ourselves to be more influenced by situational factors than we do other people because we are more aware of our own situation. This is known as the **information availability hypothesis**.

The **visual perspective hypothesis** argues that we attribute other's behavior to internal causes and our own to external causes because of our visual perspective—we view our surroundings more often than we view ourselves.

Additionally, the more information we know about another person, the more likely we are to consider situational factors when making attributions about them.

Two consequences of attribution errors are that observers are more likely to be wrong than actors when explaining the actor's behavior and observers tend to blame the victim in making judgments.

Another factor affecting attribution error is **self-serving bias**. Self-serving bias is the tendency to attribute behavior that results in a good outcome for us to internal causes and to attribute behavior that results in a bad outcome to external (situational) factors. For example, I attribute doing well on a test to the fact that I am a smart person. I attribute doing poorly on a test to the fact that I had too much other homework (the situation) and could not study sufficiently. I do not attribute poor performance to my (internal) abilities.

7.4 Interpersonal Attraction

Interpersonal attraction refers to our close relationships with others and those factors which contribute to a relationship being formed.

7.4.1 Friendship

Studies of friendships have found three factors that are important in determining who will become friends:

Similarity	People are generally attracted to those who are similar to themselves in many ways—similar in age, sex, race, economic status, etc.
Proximity or Propinquity	It is easier to develop a friendship with people who are close at hand. Proximity also increases the likelihood of repeated contacts and increased exposure can lead to increased attraction; the **mere exposure effect**. In a classic study at Massachusetts Institute of Technology, **Festinger** found that friends of women who lived in married student housing were most likely to live in the same building. In fact, half of all friends lived on the same floor.

Attractiveness	Physical attractiveness is a major factor in attraction for people of all ages. We tend to like attractive people.

7.4.2 Love

Overall, the same factors connected with friendships (i.e., similarity, proximity, and attractiveness) are also related to love relationships:

Similarity	Dating and married couples tend to be similar in age, race, social class, religion, education, intelligence, attitudes, and interests.
Proximity	We tend to fall in love with people who live nearby.
Attractiveness	We tend to fall in love with people whose attractiveness matches our own according to the **matching hypothesis**.

Researchers believe that love is a qualitatively different state than merely liking someone. Love includes physiological arousal, self-disclosure, all-encompassing interest in another individual, fantasizing about the other, and a relatively rapid swing of emotions. Unlike liking, love also includes passion, closeness, fascination, exclusiveness, sexual desire, and intense caring.

Some researchers have distinguished two main types of love:

Passionate or Romantic Love	Predominates in the early part of a romantic relationship. Includes intense physiological arousal, psychological interest, sexual desire, and the type of love we mean when we say we are "in love" with someone.
Companionate or Affectionate Love	The type of love that occurs when we have a deep, caring affection for a person.

Robert Sternberg has proposed a **triangular theory of love** that consists of three components:

Intimacy	The encompassing feelings of closeness and connectedness in a relationship.

106

| **Passion** | The physical and sexual attraction in a relationship. |
| **Decision/ Commitment** | Encompasses the initial cognition that one loves someone, and the longer-term feelings of commitment to maintain the love. |

According to Sternberg's theory, complete love only happens when all three kinds of love are represented in a relationship. Sternberg called this complete love **"consummate love."** **Fatuous love** is based on passion and commitment only and is often short-lived.

Research has shown that successful romantic relationships that last for many years are based on the expression of love and admiration, friendship between the partners, a commitment to the relationship, displays of affection, self-disclosure, and offering each other emotional support.

7.5 Social Pressure

Social pressure from others can influence our behavior.

7.5.1 Conformity

Conformity occurs when individuals adopt the attitudes or behavior of others because of real or imagined pressure.

Social norms are shared standards of behavior. People conform because they are often reinforced for conforming.

The **reciprocity norm** states that people tend to treat others as they have been treated.

Groups of people whom we are like or wish to be like are known as our **reference group**.

The classic studies of conformity were conducted by **Solomon Asch** in the 1950s. Asch demonstrated that college students will often conform with a group, even when the group adopts a position that is clearly incorrect.

Asch asked groups of college students to state which of three comparison lines matched a nearby fourth line and to make their individual responses publicly. Students were tested in groups of six. Five students in each group were hired by the experimenter to give incorrect answers. Asch found that when the first five students made the same choice, though clearly incorrect, the actual participants in the study (i.e., those not hired by the experimenter) conformed by also making this incorrect response on 37% of the trials.

Later studies showed that the tendency to conform is increased when the group is large or a person has low self-esteem. One dissenter (someone who does not conform to the group) decreases the likelihood of conformity. Some studies have found that women are more likely to conform than men.

7.5.2 Compliance

Compliance occurs when you go along with a request made of you from a person who does not have specific authority over you.

Compliance has been used to encourage people to buy things that they do not need or to do things they do not really want to do. Several different compliance techniques include:

Foot-in-the Door Technique	A two-step compliance technique in which you first ask a person to agree to a small request and later ask the person to comply with a more important or bigger one. After agreeing to the first, small request, the person has a harder time turning down the second, larger request.
Door-in-the-Face Technique	A two-step strategy that occurs by first making a request that is so large that it is certain to be denied, and then making a smaller, more reasonable request that is likely to be complied with.
Low-balling	Getting someone to agree to a commitment first and then adding disagreeable specifics later.

7.5.3 Obedience

Obedience is a form of compliance that occurs when people follow direct commands, usually from someone in a position of authority.

The classic study of obedience, using "subject-teachers" who were supposed to deliver shocks to "learners," was conducted by **Stanley Milgram**. Milgram found that a large majority of people would obey authority even if obedience caused great pain or was life-threatening to another. Milgram reported that over 85% of his subject-teachers continued to administer what they thought were painful electric shocks of 300 volts to a victim who complained of a heart condition. The vast majority of subjects (greater than 60%) also continued to obey authority and administered what they thought were the maximum, dangerous, severe shocks of 450 volts.

Even though subjects obeyed and delivered the shocks, they displayed considerable distress while doing so. They were observed to sweat, tremble, stutter, bite their lips, and groan, but they continued to administer shocks because they were told the study required them to do so. Actually, no one was shocked though the subjects thought otherwise. Today, the Milgram study would not be considered ethical because of the stress placed on the subjects.

7.6 Behavior in Groups

Social psychologists study groups as well as individuals. A **group** consists of two or more individuals who interact and are interdependent.

7.6.1 Aggression

Aggression is defined as intentionally inflicting physical or psychological harm on others.

About one-third of studies show that males are more aggressive than females, and the differences are larger with children than adults and with physical rather than verbal aggression.

The **frustration-aggression hypothesis** states that frustration produces aggression and that this aggression may be directed at the frustrater or **displaced** onto another target, as in **scapegoating**. However, frustration does not always cause aggression.

According to **social learning theory**, people learn to behave aggressively by observing aggressive models and by having their aggressive responses reinforced. For instance, parents who are belligerent with others or who use physical punishment to discipline their children tend to raise more aggressive offspring.

According to social learning theory, exposure to role models in the mass media, especially television, can influence aggression. Some research demonstrates that adults and children as young as nursery-school age show higher levels of aggression after they view media violence.

7.6.2 Altruism

Altruism or **prosocial behavior** is the selfless concern for the welfare of others that leads to helping behavior.

One of the most widely studied aspects of altruism is **bystander intervention**—whether individuals will intervene and come to the aid of a person in distress. In 1964, a young woman named **Kitty Genovese** cried out as she was being brutally murdered outside her apartment building in New York City. Thirty-eight neighbors watched and yet no one helped or even called the police. The Kitty Genovese case motivated social psychologists to study why bystanders will or will not intervene and help another individual.

The **bystander effect** states that people are less likely to help someone in an emergency situation when others are present. That is, when several people witness an emergency, each one thinks someone else will help. This appears to be due to **diffusion of responsibility**. Diffusion of responsibility is the tendency for people to feel that the responsibility for helping is shared or diffused among those who are present. The more people that are present in an emergency, therefore, the less personally responsible each individual feels. People tend to think that someone else will help or since no one is helping, possibly the person does not need help.

According to **Latane** and **Darley**, certain steps will occur before a person helps:

- They notice or observe the emergency event.

- They interpret the event as one that requires help.

- They assume responsibility for taking action. (It is here where diffusion of responsibility is likely to take place.)

- After individuals assume responsibility for helping, the decision must next be made concerning what to do.

- They take action and actually help.

Some social psychologists use a **rewards-costs approach** when explaining helping behaviors. The rewards-costs approach states that before a bystander is likely to help, the perceived rewards of helping must outweigh the costs.

Other research has found that individuals who are high in **empathy**—an emotional experience that involves a subjective grasp of another person's feelings—are more likely to help others in need. According to the **empathy-arousal hypothesis**, empathy has the power to motivate altruism.

Other factors that encourage altruism include a realization that help is necessary, being in a good mood, and seeing someone else helping.

Men are more likely to help strangers when an audience is present or when the task is especially dangerous for women. In other situations, however, men and women are equally helpful.

7.6.3 Group Processes

Psychologists also have studied how the presence of a group affects performance and decision making.

Robert Zajonc demonstrated that the presence of another person is enough to change one's performance. He proposed that we become aroused and energized when another person is around, and when we are aroused we are more likely to produce a dominant response.

Zajonc stated that on an easy or well-learned task, the dominant response is the correct response, so we will perform better and faster in the presence of another person. On a difficult task, however, the dominant response is an error, so we will perform worse and more slowly in the presence of another person.

Social facilitation is the tendency to do better on easy or well-learned tasks when another person is present.

Social loafing is a reduction in effort by individuals when they work in groups as compared to when they work by themselves. A common cause of social loafing is diffusion of responsibility—as group size increases, the responsibility for getting a job done is divided among more people, and many group members ease up because their individual contribution is less recognizable.

When people come together in groups, they often have to make decisions. Social psychologists have found some interesting tendencies in group decision making.

Risky shift is the term used to describe the fact that groups often arrive at riskier decisions than individuals do.

Deindividuation is the loss of identity as a result of being part of a large group. As a result, social restraints are lessened and impulsive or aggressive tendencies and decisions may dominate.

Group polarization occurs when group discussion strengthens a group's dominant point of view and produces a shift toward a more extreme decision.

Groupthink occurs when members of a cohesive group emphasize agreement or concurrence at the expense of critical thinking. This motivation for harmony and unanimity may result in disastrous decision making. Groupthink has been used to describe the Watergate cover-up, the escalation of the Vietnam War, and why President John F. Kennedy and his advisors could have miscalculated so badly in deciding to invade Cuba at the Bay of Pigs in 1961.

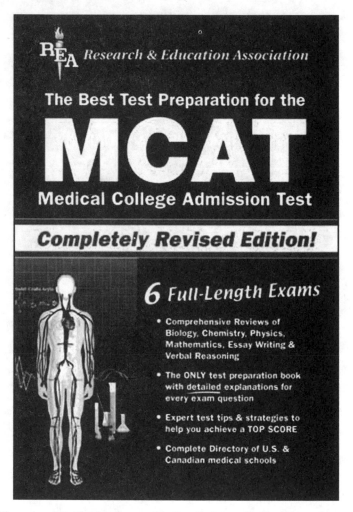

"The ESSENTIALS" of LANGUAGE

Each book in the **LANGUAGE ESSENTIALS** series offers all the essential information of the grammar and vocabulary of the language it covers. They include conjugations, irregular verb forms, and sentence structure, and are designed to help students in preparing for exams and doing homework. The **LANGUAGE ESSENTIALS** are excellent supplements to any class text or course of study.

The **LANGUAGE ESSENTIALS** are complete and concise, with quick access to needed information. They also provide a handy reference source at all times. The **LANGUAGE ESSENTIALS** are prepared with REA's customary concern for high professional quality and student needs.

Available Titles Include:

French   *Italian*

German   *Spanish*

*If you would like more information about any of these books,
complete the coupon below and return it to us or visit your local bookstore.*

MAXnotes®

REA's Literature Study Guides

MAXnotes® are student-friendly. They offer a fresh look at masterpieces of literature, presented in a lively and interesting fashion. **MAXnotes®** offer the essentials of what you should know about the work, including outlines, explanations and discussions of the plot, character lists, analyses, and historical context. **MAXnotes®** are designed to help you think independently about literary works by raising various issues and thought-provoking ideas and questions. Written by literary experts who currently teach the subject, **MAXnotes®** enhance your understanding and enjoyment of the work.

Available **MAXnotes®** include the following:

Absalom, Absalom!	Henry IV, Part I	Othello
The Aeneid of Virgil	Henry V	Paradise
Animal Farm	The House on Mango Street	Paradise Lost
Antony and Cleopatra	Huckleberry Finn	A Passage to India
As I Lay Dying	I Know Why the Caged	Plato's Republic
As You Like It	Bird Sings	Portrait of a Lady
The Autobiography of	The Iliad	A Portrait of the Artist
Malcolm X	Invisible Man	as a Young Man
The Awakening	Jane Eyre	Pride and Prejudice
Beloved	Jazz	A Raisin in the Sun
Beowulf	The Joy Luck Club	Richard II
Billy Budd	Jude the Obscure	Romeo and Juliet
The Bluest Eye, A Novel	Julius Caesar	The Scarlet Letter
Brave New World	King Lear	Sir Gawain and the
The Canterbury Tales	Leaves of Grass	Green Knight
The Catcher in the Rye	Les Misérables	Slaughterhouse-Five
The Color Purple	Lord of the Flies	Song of Solomon
The Crucible	Macbeth	The Sound and the Fury
Death in Venice	The Merchant of Venice	The Stranger
Death of a Salesman	Metamorphoses of Ovid	Sula
The Divine Comedy I: Inferno	Metamorphosis	The Sun Also Rises
Dubliners	Middlemarch	A Tale of Two Cities
The Edible Woman	A Midsummer Night's Dream	The Taming of the Shrew
Emma	Moby-Dick	Tar Baby
Euripides' Medea & Electra	Moll Flanders	The Tempest
Frankenstein	Mrs. Dalloway	Tess of the D'Urbervilles
Gone with the Wind	Much Ado About Nothing	Their Eyes Were Watching God
The Grapes of Wrath	Mules and Men	Things Fall Apart
Great Expectations	My Antonia	To Kill a Mockingbird
The Great Gatsby	Native Son	To the Lighthouse
Gulliver's Travels	1984	Twelfth Night
Handmaid's Tale	The Odyssey	Uncle Tom's Cabin
Hamlet	Oedipus Trilogy	Waiting for Godot
Hard Times	Of Mice and Men	Wuthering Heights
Heart of Darkness	On the Road	Guide to Literary Terms

RESEARCH & EDUCATION ASSOCIATION
61 Ethel Road W. • Piscataway, New Jersey 08854
Phone: (732) 819-8880   **website: www.rea.com**

Please send me more information about MAXnotes®.

Name _____

Address _____

City _____ State _____ Zip _____

REA's Test Preps
The Best in Test Preparation

- REA "Test Preps" are **far more** comprehensive than any other test preparation series
- Each book contains up to **eight** full-length practice tests based on the most recent exams
- **Every** type of question likely to be given on the exams is included
- Answers are accompanied by **full** and **detailed** explanations

REA publishes over 60 Test Preparation volumes in several series. They include:

Advanced Placement Exams (APs)
Biology
Calculus AB & Calculus BC
Chemistry
Economics
English Language & Composition
English Literature & Composition
European History
Government & Politics
Physics B & C
Psychology
Spanish Language
Statistics
United States History

College-Level Examination Program (CLEP)
Analyzing and Interpreting Literature
College Algebra
Freshman College Composition
General Examinations
General Examinations Review
History of the United States I
History of the United States II
Human Growth and Development
Introductory Sociology
Principles of Marketing
Spanish

SAT Subject Tests
Biology E/M
Chemistry
English Language Proficiency Test
French
German

SAT Subject Tests (cont'd)
Literature
Mathematics Level 1, 2
Physics
Spanish
United States History
Writing

Graduate Record Exams (GREs)
Biology
Chemistry
Computer Science
General
Literature in English
Mathematics
Physics
Psychology

ACT - ACT Assessment

ASVAB - Armed Services Vocational Aptitude Battery

CBEST - California Basic Educational Skills Test

CDL - Commercial Driver License Exam

CLAST - College Level Academic Skills Test

COOP & HSPT - Catholic High School Admission Tests

ELM - California State University Entry Level Mathematics Exam

FE (EIT) - Fundamentals of Engineering Exams - For both AM & PM Exams

FTCE - Florida Teacher Certification Exam

GED - High School Equivalency Diploma Exam (U.S. & Canadian editions)

GMAT CAT - Graduate Management Admission Test

LSAT - Law School Admission Test

MAT - Miller Analogies Test

MCAT - Medical College Admission Test

MTEL - Massachusetts Tests for Educator Licensure

NJ HSPA - New Jersey High School Proficiency Assessment

NYSTCE: LAST & ATS-W - New York State Teacher Certification

PLT - Principles of Learning & Teaching Tests

PPST - Pre-Professional Skills Tests

PSAT - Preliminary Scholastic Assessment Test

SAT

TExES - Texas Examinations of Educator Standards

THEA - Texas Higher Education Assessment

TOEFL - Test of English as a Foreign Language

TOEIC - Test of English for International Communication

USMLE Steps 1,2,3 - U.S. Medical Licensing Exams

U.S. Postal Exams 460 & 470

RESEARCH & EDUCATION ASSOCIATION
61 Ethel Road W. • Piscataway, New Jersey 08854
Phone: (732) 819-8880   **website: www.rea.com**

Please send me more information about your Test Prep books

Name _____

Address _____

City _____ State _____ Zip _____

REA's **Problem Solvers**

The "PROBLEM SOLVERS" are comprehensive supplemental textbooks designed to save time in finding solutions to problems. Each "PROBLEM SOLVER" is the first of its kind ever produced in its field. It is the product of a massive effort to illustrate almost any imaginable problem in exceptional depth, detail, and clarity. Each problem is worked out in detail with a step-by-step solution, and the problems are arranged in order of complexity from elementary to advanced. Each book is fully indexed for locating problems rapidly.

ACCOUNTING
ADVANCED CALCULUS
ALGEBRA & TRIGONOMETRY
AUTOMATIC CONTROL
   SYSTEMS/ROBOTICS
BIOLOGY
BUSINESS, ACCOUNTING, & FINANCE
CALCULUS
CHEMISTRY
COMPLEX VARIABLES
DIFFERENTIAL EQUATIONS
ECONOMICS
ELECTRICAL MACHINES
ELECTRIC CIRCUITS
ELECTROMAGNETICS
ELECTRONIC COMMUNICATIONS
ELECTRONICS
FINITE & DISCRETE MATH
FLUID MECHANICS/DYNAMICS
GENETICS
GEOMETRY
HEAT TRANSFER

LINEAR ALGEBRA
MACHINE DESIGN
MATHEMATICS for ENGINEERS
MECHANICS
NUMERICAL ANALYSIS
OPERATIONS RESEARCH
OPTICS
ORGANIC CHEMISTRY
PHYSICAL CHEMISTRY
PHYSICS
PRE-CALCULUS
PROBABILITY
PSYCHOLOGY
STATISTICS
STRENGTH OF MATERIALS &
   MECHANICS OF SOLIDS
TECHNICAL DESIGN GRAPHICS
THERMODYNAMICS
TOPOLOGY
TRANSPORT PHENOMENA
VECTOR ANALYSIS

If you would like more information about any of these books,
complete the coupon below and return it to us or visit your local bookstore.

RESEARCH & EDUCATION ASSOCIATION
61 Ethel Road W. • Piscataway, New Jersey 08854
Phone: (732) 819-8880   **website: www.rea.com**

Please send me more information about your Problem Solver books

Name _____

Address _____

City _____ State _____ Zip _____